Secret Sources of Power

Rediscovering Biblical Power Points

T. F. Tenney

and

Tommy Tenney

Fresh Bread
An Imprint of
Destiny Image® Publishers, Inc.
P.O. Box 310
Shippensburg, PA 17257-0310

ISBN 0-7684-5000-4
Library of Congress Catalog Card Number: 00-131966

For Worldwide Distribution
Printed in the U.S.A.

First Printing: 2000   Second Printing: 2000

This book and all other Destiny Image, Revival Press, MercyPlace, Fresh Bread, and Treasure House books are available at Christian bookstores and distributors worldwide.

For a U.S. bookstore nearest you, call **1-800-722-6774**.
For more information on foreign distributors, call **717-532-3040**.
Or reach us on the Internet: **http://www.reapernet.com**

Dedication

My father is one of the most powerful people I have ever known.

You would be hard pressed to find someone with stronger convictions, deeper passions, or fiercer love. The lessons my father shares in this book are principles that he has lived by—and I have been privileged to learn them not only through the words of his teachings but by the excellence of his example. Over the years, I have seen him put these principles into practice as a father, a pastor, and an apostolic leader.

Everybody wants power in their lives—but few are willing to pay the price required to tap into the greatest power of all. My father is one of those few. He knows the power of unloading and prioritizing—he has always been fond of the saying "The main thing is to keep the main thing the main thing." He is familiar with the power of forgiveness, having both extended it and received it many times over the course of his life and ministry.

It has been an honor to work with him on this book. If I have contributed anything of value to these pages, it can be attributed to the powerful, positive influence that my father has had on my life.

Thank you, Dad, for showing me the power of the Father!

—Tommy Tenney
Author, GodChaser

Acknowledgment

The authors wish to acknowledge their families who were patient and their staff who were diligent during the writing and publishing of this book.

Endorsements

It is refreshing to have a father/son book. In our day, God is joining the wisdom of age and the fire of younger men in a powerful way. The insights are practical, wise, and essential if men and women of God are to grow up into the nature of our Older Brother and Redeemer. In these pages are fundamental steps to purity and godliness—growing into maturity.

Don Finto
Director of Caleb Company
Nashville, Tennessee

It is my joyous privilege to wholeheartedly recommend this power-packed book of the Tenneys. I pray that the dynamite of truth contained within its pages will explode in the hearts and lives of multitudes, bringing life changing results.

Joy Dawson
International Bible teacher and author

Tommy Tenney has done it again! His blend of homespun stories and spiritual insights do make his writing accessible, helpful, and highly instructive.

In *Secret Sources of Power*, Tommy helps us understand the nature of God's power and how that power becomes available to us today. Scripture is full of warnings against abusing the power we've been given and Tommy pulls no punches as he draws on highly readable biblical material regarding the use and abuse of power.

This is a masterly book and one I'm glad to commend as an easy read, rooted in Scripture and vitally important as God's power fills the Church and touches the world.

Gerald Coates
Speaker, Author, Broadcaster

Do you want to be free, happy, fulfilled, and confident that you are exactly where God wants you to be? If so, I know of no better starting point than reading *Secret Sources of Power*!

C. Peter Wagner, Chancellor
Wagner Leadership Institute

I am excited about this book, *Secret Sources of Power*, for two reasons. First, the two authors collectively have experienced not merely years of ministry but many decades of walking with God with a true Caleb heart for the kingdom of God. Secondly, the combination of the two is a wonderful joining of both a vital move of the Holy Spirit today and the rich wisdom of what God has done in previous generations. It represents Jesus' encouragement for teachers to bring forth "both old and new."

To understand the heart of a true "God Chaser" it is helpful to understand his (or her) foundation. Those who know Tommy and his ministry are well aware of his deep love for both the timeless truths of the Word of God and for the timeless Truth Himself—Jesus. What many might not understand, however, is Tommy's rich heritage and upbringing in both the things of the Holy Spirit and the written Word. Just as the wisdom, insights, and experience of these two authors are priceless, so this book will be considered by all those who pray, "Teach me your ways, Lord, so that I might know you!"

Marc A. Dupont
Mantle of Praise Ministries, Inc.
Ft. Wayne, Indiana

Tommy Tenney is speaking the word of the Lord. He is on the right track for this very hour in history. His trumpet call to be "God Chasers" has sparked a fire in our land that is desperately needed. We have been filled with a fresh zeal to seek God because of his writings. All across our land people are receiving this message passionately. Bookstores keep running out of his books. My wife and kids are reading the books.

Secret Sources of Power takes you in deeper into practical applications of chasing after God. Priorities, forgiveness, and communion are vital topics Tommy addresses in these pages. You will be enriched by the "Word in season."

Billy Joe Daugherty
Victory Christian Center
Tulsa, Oklahoma

For those who have sought God and found Him, this book uncovers biblical "power points" that will help them lay aside the weights and cares of this world and find freedom in Christ.

Vinson Synan
Dean of the School of Divinity
Regent University

Israel was repeatedly warned by God not to remove the "ancient landmarks." These landmarks determined boundaries and aided the traveler seeking direction. Tommy Tenney takes us back to the ancient landmarks of biblical truth. These powerful, practical, and essential revelations will aid the spiritual pilgrim in his quest to know God and His ways. In this era of "quick fixes," greasy grace and spiritual pabulum, it's refreshing to chew on the meat of God's word. This book is a refresher course on "foundational truths"—the power of forgiveness, the power of the blood, death to self, relinquishment, etc. America will never see a sustained revival without them.

David Ravenhill
Teacher and author of
For God's Sake, Grow Up! and
They Drank From the River and Died in the Wilderness

This is a powerful book! The Tenneys have a unique gift for finding the real truth in Scripture and illuminating it for the rest of us. *Secret Sources of Power* provides insights for all believers to live a free and powerful life in Christ.

Mike Bickle
Director, International House of Prayer
Kansas City, Missouri

When people write a report about a book, they often give information about the book, and if they like it, they will end up saying, "This is a good book...get it!" I want to start with those words. *Secret Sources of Power* is a good book! I sat down to read the first chapter, and never stopped until hours later when I had finished the last chapter. If you feel "worn out" in the battle of life...if you have grieved over failures of the past, this is the book for you. The Tenneys deal with simple priorities of life and Bible foundations that will get you back on the right track...all without beating you over the head with a stick of condemnation. Here are some special things this father and son team deal with:

- Some people can't "lay aside" the weights that hold them because they can't forsake their "high powered holy-hustle" lifestyle.

- They deal with the powerful story of Martha and Mary without condemnation for either. God needs both the

"Martha" and the "Mary" among us. This revelation alone is worth the price of the book.

- Many preachers will read the material on forgiveness and preach a whole series from it. The world philosophy when you have been hurt is "Take no prisoners." The Tenneys' message: "Set them free."

- The ultimate journey of submission to God and His will brings us to the altar, "dead to sin and self but alive to God." Once we cast away the "old," and empty ourselves, we become a candidate for God's highest and most glorious intentions for us—our lives, our calling, our ministry.

Like I said...buy the book. People around you will be amazed at how knowledgeable you have become in such a short time. But we, you and I, will know the secret...*Secret Sources of Power.*

We are indebted to this father (T.F.) and son (Tommy) team. I predict we will be hearing and reading more from them. I hope it is soon.

Charles Green, Th.D., D.H.L., Litt.D.
Founding pastor, Faith Church
New Orleans, Louisiana

A double hitter by father and son! Here are life changing insights that help us tap into God's power, thereby striking out the enemy.

Jane Hansen
President / CEO, Aglow International

Often we are not cognizant of the power of God that resides in the simplest of spiritual truths. In *Secret Sources of Power,* Tommy Tenney and T.F. Tenney make fresh these simple truths. He reminds us of the unlimited power available to us when we put into action all of God's instructions. Tommy is a "living epistle" of everything he writes. The principles he so avidly embraces come alive and empower you while reading this book!

Kingsley A. Fletcher
Senior pastor, Life Community Church
Research Triangle Park, North Carolina

This is a high impact combination—father and son preparing the way for revival. Both are passionate, inspirational ministers and choice servants of God. Together, they are able to bridge generational and denominational chasms and gaps. This fact alone carries a potent message! Add to that the rich content of *Secret Sources of Power* and you have combustible material for the fire of God to ignite your heart, family, and church. These men and their writings are another gift from God to take the worldwide Church to the next spiritual level.

Sergio Scataglini
President, Scataglini Ministries, Inc.

Tommy Tenney has brought us biblical truths, with some rare insights and godly wisdom, reminding us of what is required for those who would be alive in the saving power of Jesus Christ. This is a wonderful book.

Dr. Ché Ahn
Harvest Rock Church
President of Harvest International Ministries

Wonderful writing! New insights into important topics! While others have written on some of these themes, our friend Tommy Tenney gives forth the profound insights born of a man who is deeply passionate for the Lord himself. No one should be able to read this book without significant benefit.

Dan Juster
Director, Tikkun Ministries, Inc.
Gaithersburg, Maryland

This book is a roll call of life-giving principles. Page after page, Tommy Tenney and T.F. Tenney skillfully highlight the tools we need to apply to be perfectly free in Christ.

Ted Haggard
Senior Pastor, New Life Church
Colorado Springs, Colorado

I had a rough time getting through *Secret Sources of Power*. I would read and weep. Reap and worship. Read and repent. Read and pray. Read and get so ravenous to know what the Word had to say on the particular subject that I would be happily lost for hours on righteous rabbit trails.

I remember thinking, *What is it about a Tenney book?*

Immediately the familiar Voice whispered, "It's My book, that's what there is about it!"

Secret Sources of Power is not a fast food snack you inhale as you race through life. No...it's a spiritual Epicurean feast. Tantalizing appetizers. Hearty soups. Fresh-baked bread. Melt-in-your-mouth slow roasted prime meats. Garden-grown, vine-ripened vegetables. Just-picked aromatic herbs. Succulent sauces. Peak harvest. Juicy ripe fruits. Honey-laced savories. Rich sweet cream. Ice-cold artesian spring water and two-thousand-year-old vintage New Wine.

Hungry yet?

Dr. Reba Rambo-McGuire
Revivalist, Rambo McGuire Ministries
Nashville, Tennessee

I am an avid sermon notetaker, but somewhere during my second Tommy Tenney service, I abandoned my notetaker's journal and decided to buy the tape instead. The reason? I couldn't keep up with him. Tommy is the prince of quotable quotes, encapsulating more truth, revelation and anointing into potent, unforgettable one-liners than most of us preachers can say in a whole message.

When I read *Secret Sources of Power*, co-written with his father, it became obvious that Tommy has the same testimony as Jesus: "When you've seen the son, you've seen the father."

I devoured *Secret Sources of Power* in one sitting. This powerful book should be required reading for new converts and the spiritually mature alike. Every chapter could be a stand-alone book. I can't wait for the Tenneys' next installment. They are an extraordinary father and son who are richly blessing Christendom with the wisdom, anointing and intimacy with Jesus gleaned only from many years of beholding His glory.

Judy A. Gossett
Worshiper, The River
Vancouver, British Columbia, Canada

Contents

Foreword by T. F. Tenney

Power. The dictionary definition reads: "The ability or capacity to perform or act effectively." As an old-fashioned apostolic minister of the Gospel, I have gleaned the chapters you hold in your hand from various sermons I have preached through the years. There is a timelessness about their content and "the ability and capacity to perform or act effectively" that comes as Bible principles are instituted in the lives of men and women who are committed to the Christ of the cross.

As the human mind courses through the sandy loam, the red clay, and the black topsoil of its environment, undoubtedly it picks up portions of each. Wherever possible, I have given due credit to authors and sources. Recognize that what you read here is the product of my experience with God, personal research, and exposure to godly men and women. I have attempted to give credit when sources were known. However, if I missed something along the way, please understand it was not intentional but simply the product of nearly fifty years of ministry and making the work and words of others a part of who I am...a fellow traveler, pursuing Him who is the secret source of power.

Introduction by Tommy Tenney

The search for power is as old as time itself, yet as current as today's newspaper. It shapes individuals and shakes nations. From schoolyard scuffles to nuclear arms, this quest touches us in every stage of life regardless of our location, socioeconomic status, or position.

Man's use and abuse of power is chronicled in our history books, enshrined in our monuments, and glamorized in our legends. It is taught in our schools and promised in our pulpits. Commercials preach that certain products will empower us, or threaten that lack of the same will leave us powerless. We have power lunches, power naps, and power bars—but even in this energized environment, true power often eludes us.

Secret Sources of Power will take you down a road less traveled. You will re-discover that the way up is down; to lay hold you must let go; to be filled you must become empty. *It isn't the easy way*...but if you want a power that doesn't rise and fall with circumstance and whim, *it is the only way*!

Part I

The Power of Unloading

*Therefore we also, since we are surrounded by so great a cloud of witnesses, **let us lay aside every weight**, and the sin which so easily ensnares us, and let us run with endurance the race that is set before us, looking unto Jesus, the author and finisher of our faith, who for the joy that was set before Him endured the cross, despising the shame, and has sat down at the right hand of the throne of God (Hebrews 12:1-2).*

Chapter 1

Unload the Weight of Life and the Pressing Demands of Other People

Have you ever observed professional horse racing? Did you notice the size of the jockeys? The owners make every effort to reduce the weight their racehorse must carry—that means they want small, light riders. The effect of this "unloading" is so great that if a jockey is too light, then race officials consider it an unfair advantage! They fit a special pouch to the rider's saddle loaded with weights to "even out" the race.

Paul wrote to the Hebrews urging them, "...let us lay aside every weight, and the sin which so easily ensnares us, and let us run with endurance the race that is set before us" (Heb. 12:1).

I have to wonder if some of us are trying to run our race in Christ while carrying overstuffed suitcases. Even worse, some of us are staggering down the course with a top-heavy stack of baggage so high we can't even see where we are going!

Satan does everything he can to overload us with the baggage of the world and the entangling cares of life. God, on the other hand, wants us to unload everything He never gave us in the first place. He promises to help us bear our burden, but only if it is *His burden*:

Come to Me, all you who labor and are heavy laden, and I will give you rest. Take My yoke upon you and learn from Me, for I am gentle and lowly in heart, and you will find rest for your souls. For My yoke is easy and My burden is light (Matthew 11:28-30).

God promises us He will not allow us to be loaded with more than we can bear.[1] Life is filled with contradictions and complexities, but there are generally two kinds of "weight" that find their way onto our shoulders: the weight that comes to us through life, circumstances, and other people; and the weight we pile on ourselves.

Don't Focus on Things You Cannot Change

There will always be people or things (such as company policies, government regulations, court decisions, or unfair zoning ordinances) that will actively oppose your walk with Christ. You are unlikely to change many of these sources of opposition apart from God's intervention. If you focus on them, you will lose your focus on the Lord. Inevitably, you will become weary and faint.

What is the solution? Consider Him. Keep your mind focused on Him. Instead of pondering the things and people opposing you, keep your mind on Jesus Christ and the things of God. If you "stew" over things you cannot readily change, you are bound to end up with heartburn (physically *and* spiritually).

Your Lord knows all about opposition. He endured it personally. The apostle Paul followed up his statements about "laying aside every weight" with a powerful perspective correction:

*For **consider Him** who endured such hostility from sinners against Himself, lest you become weary and discouraged in your souls. You have not yet resisted to bloodshed, striving against sin* (Hebrews 12:3-4).

Can you imagine anything more ludicrous than that the sinless Lamb of God would take on Himself all the sins of the world just to save the human race? Then to have those same human beings conspire together to kill Him, to have the leaders of the Jewish nation conspire with leaders of the Gentile world to name Him a criminal and murder Him by crucifixion on a cross? Now that is a contradiction! Yet, Jesus Christ endured it for us.

Set Christ Before You and Endure

Now He wants us to remember Him as we face the contradictions and challenges of life. This is the way to endure and not grow weary or fainthearted. The Bible says that when Jesus endured the cross, He did it "for the joy that was set before Him..." (Heb. 12:2b). His joy was at least twofold: He anticipated the joy of pleasing His Father, and He anticipated the joy of seeing millions of lost people coming into the Kingdom of God.

Frustration over things you don't understand can quickly weigh you down. We serve a God who speaks worlds into existence with a single command. He is not prone to providing explanations for the endless questions we send His way. If it isn't in His Word already, and if He doesn't answer a question through His Spirit, we are left with an unanswered "why" to deal with. David asks "why" at least 29 times in the *New King James Version* of the Psalms, and God called him "a man after My own heart, who will do all My will" (Acts 13:22b). Be encouraged: You are not the first individual whose mind is filled with "whys." The biggest room in your brain should be reserved for "Things I Do Not Understand."

Sometimes you have to "unload" some weight before you can take on any more. Life gets difficult when we give too much "weight" to the things we cannot change in life. The first thing we should do is make sure we aren't carrying the weight of any sin in our lives.

The redemptive blood of Jesus Christ cleanses us from all sin. Even though we want to lay aside every weight, we sometimes fail to comprehend God's power to forget. In other words, we carry the effects of sin with us when technically, they are no longer ours to bear. Once we cast them into the "sea of forgetfulness," they are only as effective in our lives as we allow them to be. We must accept God's full forgiveness and lay aside our sins and failures forever.

If the enemy cannot ensnare you in an overt or illegitimate way by tempting you to commit some sin of commission, then he will try to ensnare you in a "legitimate" way—through sins of *omission*. Either way, we take care of sins through repentance. Someone once boasted to me, "I don't need to repent!" My response to him was, "You need to repent for feeling like you don't need to repent!"

Lay Aside Everything That Weighs You Down

We all need to repent. It is the biblical way to *"lay aside every weight, and the sin which so easily ensnares us."* You "get down to the real you" by taking off the facades and setting aside the weights. According to an edition of the Bible containing comparative passages from up to 26 different translations, this passage in Hebrews 12:1 reads: *"stripping off every encumbrance"* (Rotherham's translation), or *"Let us fling aside every encumbrance,"* (Weymouth's translation). The Williams translation says it a little stronger: *"Let us throw off every impediment."* The 20th Century translation says, *"Let us lay aside everything that hinders us,"* while the Knox translation reads, *"Let us rid ourselves of all that weighs us down."*[2]

Some things in life may not stop you, but they will slow you down. The enemy will always settle for second best. *If he cannot stop you from serving Christ, then **slowing you down** is the next best thing.* If he can weigh you down enough to make you walk out your race instead of running it, then he has won at least a partial victory.

We live in a high-tech, high-paced, non-stop age. A hundred years ago, if you missed the stagecoach, there would be another one the next month. Today, if we miss one plane or phone call, we fear it can put us off schedule for six weeks. Our schedules themselves can become major hindrances in our lives.

The Enemy Wants to Wear You Out

Daniel the prophet said that in the end times, the anti-Christ would *"wear out* the saints of the Most High...."* (Dan. 7:25b KJV). The spirit of anti-Christ is at work in the world right now, and it comes against us in the form of little things that keep weighing on us. They drain our creative energies and work to rob us of spiritual integrity unit by unit. These things don't quite qualify as sin—they are just unnecessary weights. The power to run, the power to endure, and the power to stay focused rests with our ability to unload those encumbering, entangling weights. It begins with the wisdom of knowing what to take on and what to let go.

Children need to learn two principles when they are young. First, they need to learn the principle of discipline: Life is not doing what you want to do; it is doing what you ought to do. Secondly, they should learn the principle of priorities: Your relationship with God is the single most important relationship in your life. Second is family; and third is your ministry and calling. We must encourage them—and ourselves—to set godly priorities and discipline themselves to follow them.

Improper priorities can quickly overload us with duties, commitments, and projects that lead far from where we belong. The greatest danger is that "the temporal" will crowd out "the eternal."

Very few church problems are based on eternal issues. The problems usually stem from disagreements about minor "temporal" or non-eternal things such as: "my money," "my piano," "my church," "my rights...." Very few church meetings turn contentious over questions of false doctrine, but countless church congregations have split after disagreeing about minor money disbursement decisions, church decorations, and even the placement of coat racks in the foyer!

Come Apart in Prayer or Fall Apart

We tend to be more "problem conscious" than "power conscious." Perhaps this is why Jesus instructed His disciples on one occasion to come aside or come apart for a while.[3] If you don't "come apart for a little while," then you might "fall apart for a long while." Jesus set the example for us by taking time to "unload" in the presence of His Father.

*Satan has made it **his priority** to keep the saints of God from **their priorities**.* He does his best to keep us so bogged down in "things" that we forget to spend time with God. As a result, we are driven by debt, fear, and loneliness. Pharaoh and the taskmasters of Egypt attempted to wear out the children of Israel; in our day, the enemy increases our "Egyptian" responsibilities hoping to do the same thing. We must learn and apply the principles of "unloading" so we can decrease the enemy's ability to overload us. If you don't unload, you will definitely overload (and maybe even blow a fuse!).

David found himself in that proverbial spot "between a rock and a hard place" the day he returned to Ziklag with his fighting men to find their homes in flames and every single member of their families gone. His men talked of killing David. The crops and animals were gone, their homes were nothing but burning embers, wives and children were gone, and no one knew who took them nor where they went. The missing family members could be dead for all they knew.

He Took Time Off for a Prayer Meeting

David didn't have a nervous breakdown or take on the unnecessary weight of personal guilt over something he didn't cause and couldn't change. He said, "Give me the prayer shawl. Bring me that old ephod."[4] He got under that prayer shawl and said to himself, "I've got to talk to God!" Can you imagine how that looked to his fighting men? In the midst of absolute chaos and emotional ruin, this man just shut down everything and went to prayer. Even though an unknown enemy appeared to be running off with everything he owned and every person he loved, David took time off for a prayer meeting. Did he know something we don't know?

Everything was stacked against David; the sounds of discontent and despair filled the air around him. Yet he thought, *I can't listen to this anymore. I have to get a sure word from the Lord Jehovah.* In a time of desperate crisis, David was distressed and hurt; but he didn't load up with sorrow, anger, and despair. *He unloaded.* He prayed until he got his word from the Lord. It was a simple instruction and promise, but it was enough: *"Pursue them. I am with you. You're not going to lose a thing. Here's the plan...."*[5]

TOO OFTEN WE PANIC WHEN WE OUGHT TO PRAY; WE FAINT WHEN WE OUGHT TO "FAITH."

What if David didn't know when or how to unload? What would you do if you found yourself in David's situation? *Too often we panic when we ought to pray; we faint when we ought to "faith."* This isn't a matter of "faking" it—*it is a time to "FAITH" it!* This is the power that comes with unloading.

The enemy has no power to harm you in and of himself. He gets his power from *you* when you release it to him! However, when you unload your own preconceived notions of power and responsibility and give yourself to Christ, the Holy Spirit is released by you and through you.

What do you do when life shows up and God doesn't? You focus on Him anyway and unload the situation into His care. Peter, Jesus' most impetuous disciple, wrote in his later and more mature years, "[Cast] all your care upon Him, for He cares for you" (1 Pet. 5:7).

There Are Some Burdens You Cannot Unload

When we talk about the power of unloading, we also need to realize there are burdens we are *supposed to bear* as part of our responsibilities in the family of God. The Bible tells us to *"bear* **one another's** *burdens,"* in one place, and to *"bear* [your] **own** *load"* in another (Gal 6:2a and 5b, respectively). Some people think everybody has to help them carry their burden; others refuse to help anyone else based on the belief that no one should be a burden on others. The truth is in the middle of these two extremes as described above in God's Word. Each of us must bear our own burden *and* help others who are in need. In those times when our burden seems too heavy to bear alone, we shouldn't be too proud to ask for help from the Body of Christ.

God permits certain things to come into our lives for a divine purpose. We know that He is not the author of sickness, disease, death, or evil; and we also know that His plans for us are always good. He said, "For I know the thoughts that I think toward you, says the Lord, thoughts of peace and not of evil, to give you a future and a hope" (Jer. 29:11). However, He does allow us to go through difficulties or face challenges that are not "weights" to be laid aside. They are valleys we must walk through with the Lord at our side.

Someone might say, "I'm climbing a rough, rough mountain." Be thankful! If it weren't rough, it would be virtually impossible to climb because you can't climb a smooth mountain— there are no outcroppings to hold on to. The very things we think are sent to destroy us are often sent to conform us to Christ's image. They come into our lives to build spiritual strength.

Tests and trials often come into our lives to help us learn a crucial lesson in our walk with God. How will you ever *know* that "He who is in you is greater than he who is in the world" (1 Jn. 4:4b), if you don't overcome a temptation through the supernatural power of His Spirit within you?

The gospel will change you. It is the power of God unto salvation. Don't become bogged down in the bondage of the familiar and miss the presence of God right in front of you. Avoid becoming a victim of "form without function," a member of a local church who has the outward form of godliness but denies the power of the God who created the Church.[6]

Disaster or Miracle? Follow the Spirit!

Some of the most embarrassing moments in a minister's life may be those times when he or she tried to "rebuke" something only to find out that it was God at work. Form must always follow function. Many local churches expect the Holy Spirit to conform to their order of service, printed church schedule, or pre-established agendas; when all of those outward forms should follow the leading of the Spirit. Many times, what we think is the beginning of a disaster will actually be the beginning of a miracle! This happens most often when we fail to discern the seasons of the Lord. There are times to hold on and there are times to let things go. In the same way, there is a time and a season for "unloading."

Jonathan made a spiritual covenant with David and their hearts were knit together. Yet he also had a physical covenant with his father. He was torn between his loyalty to his spiritual brother and his biological father, King Saul. When he followed the flesh instead of the spiritual, early death came to him.[7] He could not discern what to hold and what to unload.

Finally, we must realize that before there can be a filling, there has to be an emptying. It is hard for God to fill a person who is already running over with "self." He can't give you solutions when you are clinging to your problems and refuse to unload them.

Sometimes we have to unload the assignments we cannot accomplish by ourselves. God told the prophet Elijah to do three specific tasks, but he only accomplished one of those assignments—the anointing of Elisha.[8] God passed the remaining assignments on to Elisha after Elijah was caught up into heaven. Elijah felt the burden of three generations during his ministry. God knew Elijah could not fulfill all three tasks, so He just transferred the burden to another. You will always sense the "burden of the unfulfilled" if you are part of God's eternal purpose. Just remember there are times when you must release your burden to future generations.

When you sense there are eternal things you will never accomplish in your lifetime, you have a choice: You can become frustrated by it, or you can realize that things are either *timely* or *timeless*. God speaks both into our hearts. Our job is to know what to unload, what to fulfill, and what to pass on.

There will be times when you simply need to unload. Get with God, rest in the Father, worship Jesus, and walk in the Spirit. Love Him. Serve Him. Do your best to please Him, and remember that if something pleases God, it doesn't matter who it displeases. If it displeases Him, it doesn't matter who else is pleased.

If you want God to infuse you with last-day revival power, then understand that first you may need to unload some things in your life. He may be waiting for you to get rid of some things to make room for Him. Do you love Him beyond everything and everyone else? Do you love Him more than any problem or position in your life? Do you focus on Him more than the distractions in your life? Is He greater than every failure and disappointment you have experienced? Lay aside the weights...lay aside the sins that so easily entangle you...*consider Him.* This is the first step on the road to power.

Endnotes

1. See 1 Cor. 10:13.

2. All the translations noted are cited in *26 Translations of the NEW TESTAMENT*, Curtis Vaughan, gen. ed. (Oklahoma City, Oklahoma: Mathis Publishers—Copyright 1967 by Zondervan Publishing House, Grand Rapids, Michigan), p. 1107.

3. See Mk. 6:31.

4. See 1 Sam. 30:6-7.

5. See 1 Sam. 30:8.

6. See 2 Tim. 3:5.

7. See 1 Sam. 31:2.

8. See 1 Kings 19:15-16.

Chapter 2

Unload Your Self-imposed Weights and Entanglements

God created each of us to carry specific kinds and sizes of "loads" in life. In every case, He intends for us to carry more than just "our load" in life. This is what John meant when he wrote, "By this we know love, because He laid down His life for us. And we also ought to lay down our lives for the brethren" (1 Jn. 3:16). It is one of the most important ways we can demonstrate that we are created in His image and likeness, and are filled with His presence.

The problem is that if we *overload ourselves* with self-imposed limitations, personal problems, and financial dilemmas, then He cannot add anything to our load. Frankly, His Kingdom suffers when we are too selfish to pick up His cross and do as He does. He says, "I cannot put My burden on you; it will break you. I will withhold the 'burden of the Lord' from you." The only way we can receive His burden[1] and accomplish His purpose is to discover and activate the power of unloading.

There are things in life that you must simply choose to forget. It is easier to deal with a man who has a poor memory than with a man who has a poor "forgetter." Have you encountered people who could not forget wrongs they suffered decades earlier? They often stand out because they have allowed bitterness over some real or imagined wrong to color and distort 20 or 30 years of their lives!

The problem is that their "forgetter" is broken. They are so thoroughly enmeshed and entangled in their hurt that they never allow God to heal the wound. This is what the apostle Paul called a "besetting" or ensnaring sin and weight.[2]

The Job of Unloading Is in Your Portfolio, Not God's!

Many times these people will say, "I've asked God to take it away and He just won't." You could tell them the truth and say, "No, God said for *you* to do it. The Scripture says, '...let *us* lay aside every weight' (Heb. 12:1a). The job is in your portfolio, not God's." However, don't be surprised if they reply, "I've tried that. I just can't...."

God would not tell us to "lay aside" something if we were not fully capable of doing it. It is not that we *cannot*; it is that we *will not*. We have established habits and imposed things upon ourselves that have nothing to do with the gospel. ·

Balanced priorities are essential. Some of us tend to become consumed with the work of God while actually neglecting our *relationship* with Him. We get so busy doing the things of God that we sacrifice our walk with God. No one was more dedicated to do the will of God than His Son Jesus. Yet, even though the whole world was lost in darkness, the Bible tells us that Jesus "came apart to rest" or went away from the crowds to be alone for a time.[3] We need to follow His example, especially when a problem or situation threatens to consume our lives.

It is significant that the first administrative decision of the New Testament church leadership was that the apostles, or those in the "feeding and leading" ministry, were to give themselves to prayer and the Word. They assigned someone else to provide daily care for the widows. The apostles made sure it was done, by delegating the work so it wouldn't become a weight that hindered the propagation of the gospel message to the world.

We can be sure pressure will come at times, but we always face the same choice: pressure or priorities? *You will never come into a dimension of God's power until you learn how to prioritize and unload.* Many things in life will come along to deter you from your goal or slow your progress. Nevertheless, God's thermometer stays fixed; the labels on His bottles don't change with circumstances. He is "the same yesterday, today, and forever" (Heb. 13:8). His prescription for health in good times and hard times hasn't changed: "Therefore I exhort first of all that supplications, prayers, intercessions, and giving of thanks be made for all men" (1 Tim. 2:1).

The most popular excuse you hear is, "I just don't have time." Yet all of us are given the same number of hours each day. Each of us has 1,440 minutes to "spend" each day. We decide how to use the 86,400 seconds per day, and our management of that time makes all the difference. Some things must be set aside for later, and some things must be unloaded altogether.

Exchange Your Weights for Power to Run the Race

Are there weights in your life—things you've taken upon yourself—that are not the burden of the Lord? He wants you to lay them aside in exchange for power to run the race! Unnecessary weights will weary your mind and turn you into a zombie in the spiritual world.

God's Word says you can take care of that by unloading or flinging off that weight. If it's a sin, repent of it. If it is a weight or care you have brought on yourself, lay it aside. Are you over-loaded with the unrealistic expectations of others? Unload them before you become a slave in the "Kingdom of They-dom." The bottom line is that "the government is on His shoulder," not the shoulders of your critics or would-be slave drivers.[4] Please God before you please man.

Have you noticed that whenever you set out to do something for the Lord, it seems like the enemy paints a target on your shield? It is easy to get overloaded when this happens because if the enemy can't get to you by one means, he always tries anoth-er. If you feel worn down and short-circuited like a battery that has run dry, then try the power that comes with unloading! Set your priorities and let Him determine your load.

God made us with two ends—one to think with, the other to sit on. The end you use determines whether you win or lose: Heads you win, tails you lose! Trite as it may sound, if you are so overloaded and burdened with things not of God that you virtu-ally "cannot move," then you will lose. Use your head. Learn the power of unloading and give your burdens to the Lord. Then we can accept the "burden of the Lord" and share the yoke with Jesus. He makes the burden easy to bear, and when He shares the burden, losers become winners every time![5]

Much of the excess "weight" we place on our souls comes from wrong thinking. This is one of the enemy's strongholds and negative thinking is his by-product. He wants you to be overbur-dened about things you cannot change. That is why the Bible instructs us to bring "every thought into captivity to the obedi-ence of Christ" (2 Cor. 10:5b).

Unload the Impossible and Experience the Supernatural

It is hard to unload a problem and look to God when you believe you have no power to change it. Let God have it anyway.

It is the only way you can discover the power of unloading. You haven't lived until you unload an impossible problem only to find yourself irrevocably tied to a Kingdom enterprise that seems even more impossible—and then watch it unfold before your eyes. By the time you emerge from that God-adventure, your "problem" won't seem so big in comparison to your supernatural God.

Many "modern" saints are discovering that the "tyranny of the urgent" can easily crowd out the really important things of life. Everything seems to be "urgent" in the new millennium. You rush to get an urgent phone call, you break records to deliver urgent responses. No matter what is said over the phone or comes across your desk in memo form, it is *"URGENT."*

If God has an enemy in the typical local church today, it really isn't the devil. It is the one-word enemy, "Hurry." No matter how much of a "high-powered, holy-hustle" rush you find yourself in, the Book still says, "Those who wait on the Lord shall renew their strength" (Is. 40:31a). This is another source of secret power. God only promises to renew the waiters—the people who have learned to lay aside and unload other things so they can wait on Him. Learn to wait on God until He hears and answers you.

Can God Interrupt Your Schedule?

Think about all the "baggage" you carry around with you. Ask yourself, "Is all this necessary?" It may be legitimate, but it is still a weight, nonetheless. Schedules have become our slave-drivers and we have become "must do list" addicts! We are afraid to do anything or go anywhere without first checking our palm PCs, appointment books, electronic organizers, or on-line time management programs. Ask yourself: "Can God interrupt me? Have I made it impossible for the Almighty to get my attention without triggering a major catastrophe or sending fire down from Heaven?"

We need to stay open to divine interruption at any time. Some of the greatest "God experiences" in our lives can happen when we have something else planned. Pray that when God interrupts your schedule, you will be sensitive enough to realize it is God and obey Him rather than your appointment book! If you decide to pursue your own agenda instead of Him, don't be surprised if you "run into a brick wall" and wake up with a headache saying, "Oh, God. *What went wrong?*" His response will be simple, "You did. You went wrong when you didn't inquire of Me and seek My face."

The New Testament portrait of Mary and Martha responding to Jesus' visit to their home in Bethany reveals an important principle at work. Both of them were needed. Mary knew how to minister to the divinity of Christ, and she gave it top priority. Martha knew how to minister to His humanity and that was her primary focus. When you get both of these ministries operating in unity in the same house, there is power. Yet there must be balance.

SOMEWHERE IN THE MIDDLE OF MARTHA'S KITCHEN AND MARY'S SEAT OF DEVOTION AT JESUS' FEET THERE IS A PLACE OF DIVINE POWER.

Martha was so encumbered by her focus on ministry in the natural that she was blind to the priority of the spiritual. She made it difficult for the Spirit to interrupt her kitchen agenda of serving the Lord's natural needs for the sake of the spiritual. On the other hand, Mary was so "heavenly minded" that at times she bordered on the neglectful. If Martha hadn't been there, she would have kept Jesus talking long after dinnertime and into the night without a meal.

Forced to choose between the two, the Lord will always choose the one who sits at His feet in adoration and communes with Him. He will always put footwashers before food-preparers, but He prefers to have *both*. Somewhere in the middle of Martha's kitchen and Mary's seat of devotion at Jesus' feet there is a place of divine power. The ideal balance would place both Mary and Martha at Jesus' feet in joyful devotion and communion until the appropriate time; then both would be released in power to serve Him and worship Him in the "kitchen" of life.

We must not be guilty of putting the secondary above the primary. Our primary purpose in life is to praise and worship God. We are called to be worshipers long before any of us are called to be "ministers of the gospel." (After we lay down our earthly bodies, we will lay down every secondary call, in order to praise and worship Him unceasingly.) It is possible to succeed in the secondary and fail in the primary, but this is not "true success" by eternity's measure.

All of us must deal with this balance between our primary "worship" calling and our secondary "ministry" calling. We never "graduate" from our worship ministry; we simply become qualified to carry an additional—and secondary—load from God.

We Shift the Burden We Share
With God to Our Shoulders Alone

When we take our eyes off Him—even at the height of our earthly ministry—we can quickly become overloaded by a burden that is "easy" when it is borne on a shared yoke with God. When we look away from the Master, as Peter did while walking on the water, we immediately begin to sink into what was solid only seconds earlier.[6] A "temporary amnesia" seems to strike, causing us to think we are going through life alone. In that moment, we unconsciously shift the burden of ministry from the yoke we share with God to our shoulders alone (with disastrous results).

In one day's time, Elijah the prophet experienced both the highest point in his ministry and the lowest point in his entire life. He boldly challenged 450 prophets of Baal to a public showdown on Mount Carmel. He kept his focus in the midst of the thunderous shouts, screams, and agonizing groans of the 450 prophets as they tried in vain to call down fire from their false god.

Elijah was unmoved by the thousands of skeptical and hostile onlookers encircling him. He had heard from the living God, so with supernatural calm and confidence, three times he ordered that gallon after gallon of water be poured over the wood of his altar of sacrifice until it filled a trench encircling the altar.

With unwavering voice, Elijah the prophet called upon Jehovah in front of his enemies and the fire of God consumed the sacrifice, the wood, the twelve stones of the altar, and even licked up the water in the trench! Elijah quickly ordered the awestruck crowd to seize the priests of Baal and he personally executed them. Finally, after a long day of spiritual warfare in the hot sun, Elijah lifted up his long robes and outran King Ahab's chariot to the gate of Jezreel and waited while the king told Queen Jezebel everything Elijah had done!

Elijah Looked Away to Consider Jezebel's Threats and Forgot God

In a matter of moments, Elijah the prophet received a single-sentence message from Jezebel that made him shake like a leaf! That temporary amnesia seemed to strike when Elijah "looked away" to *consider the threats* of Jezebel the "prophet killer" and forgot the God he served (I Kings 19:2,3).

How could Elijah forget everything God had done that day? The fire from Heaven faded from memory. Somehow he forgot about the power God had shown through him to transform thousands of doubters into believers that day. All he wanted to do in that moment of stark fear was to *run away from the woman he feared* as fast as he could.

This man had single-handedly defeated all the bloodthirsty priests of Baal in a supernatural showdown only hours earlier. How could he run from the threats of one woman and hide under a juniper tree like a frightened child? It is dangerous to turn our focus away from God. Elijah never fully recovered from his fear that day. Even though God took him into Heaven with Himself, never again did Elijah return to the cutting edge of what God was doing in his day.

Other leaders in the Bible also failed to "unload" and suffered setbacks and failures because of it. David was at least 50 years old when he committed adultery with Bathsheba and plotted the murder of her husband (who was also one of David's "mighty men" and a trusted body guard). He and Bathsheba lost their baby, and David's sin carried on into his family line.

Solomon, the second son Bathsheba bore him, was fine until he also fell into sexual sin. He encumbered himself with seven hundred wives and three hundred concubines—many of whom worshiped false gods and successfully encouraged Solomon to do the same.

Where David had several wives and a single sexual sin, Solomon took his father's indulgence to the extreme. The sins, weights, and encumbrances permitted to remain in one generation will often increase exponentially in the next. The only way to break such a generational curse is through the power of the Holy Ghost. Release the power of unloading by transferring the weight of the generational sins of the past onto the broad shoulders of the God of your past, your present, and your future.

Set the Example for Tomorrow's Generation: Unload Now

We must unload every sin and weight *now* so the generations of tomorrow will be filled with faith and power. Let us raise up a generation of men and women who walk in the Spirit of God with the manifestation of supernatural power, not willful weakness and sin. Set the example for tomorrow's generation by releasing the power of unloading today!

In many instances, the things we allow to hinder and defeat us are based on imaginary wrongs or simple misunderstandings that could easily be resolved. One man said something had happened 27 years earlier in his life that left him embittered and resentful toward another person. For nearly three decades, he lived in misery and bitterness until the conviction of God led him to go to the man he felt had wronged him. The man knew nothing about the incident because he never said the things that allegedly caused the offense! That meant that for 27 years, this brother had carried the stifling weight of an imaginary incident around his neck. He let bitterness lodge in his spirit by failing to lay aside the weight of offense.

When the apostle Paul wrote, *"Who will deliver me from this body of death?"* (Rom. 7:24) he was referring to something very similar to the experience of the man we just discussed. Did you know that crucifixion was not the worst form of Roman execution? The Romans went one step further into horror by fastening the corpse of a dead man to the body of a living person condemned to die. Arm was tied to arm, leg to leg, torso to torso and so forth. Then the living man was forced to carry the rotting corpse with him day and night until the putrefaction of the decaying body ate into the body of the living to kill its host.

Paul was saying, "I was carrying around something dead, but God cut it loose from me and saved my life." God has cut away the dying remains of your past sins, failures, and weaknesses and given you a new life with a new name and identity. Why should you pick up those dead remains again? It must be unloaded before it begins to destroy you. You cannot be a part of a fresh move of God while you are tied to a rotting corpse from the past. Unload it on God and let Him deliver you from it forever. For the new man to live in you, you must be cut loose from the old things weighing you down.

Don't waste the years of your life on bitterness over an old wound or an incident that may have never even happened. If you suffer a wound or hurt in the course of life, don't let the wound fester. The Bible instructs us to "agree with our adversaries quickly," which means we should settle things quickly.[7]

Sit Up All Night, But Don't Go to Bed Angry

This is good advice for friendships and married couples. Work through your misunderstandings honestly and settle your differences quickly. "Do not let the sun go down on your wrath" (Eph. 4:26b). Perhaps you have heard mature Christian couples say, "We don't argue, but we do have 'intense fellowship' sometimes." One fellow said his marriage had lasted 50 plus years because he and his wife had an agreement not to ever go to bed angry with each other. Then he added with a twinkle in his eye, "Of course, there have been some nights we sat up all night...." Deal with differences and wounds honestly and without delay. Tap the power of unloading to transfer the weight of offenses and wrongs to God so you can be healed and remain whole.

All the ministries in the world will not be able to lift you, if you are overloaded with self-imposed problems and limitations. Remember that Jesus said, "My yoke is easy and My burden is light" (Mt. 11:30).

Sooner or later someone will disappoint or fail you in some way. Don't allow that hurt to become a bitter place in your heart. Let it go, lay it aside, unload it at Jesus' feet.

Rediscover the "unloading power" of "child-likeness." Jesus said, "...unless you are converted and become as little children, you will by no means enter the kingdom of Heaven" (Mt. 18:3). The Greek word translated as "become" means to "*continually* become." In other words, this is a continual unending process. Yes, there is a difference between childishness and *"child-likeness."* Just as you can be "wise as a serpent and gentle as a dove," so you can be both "child-like" and "mature" at the same time. No one should stop learning after mastering their ABC's. It still takes a working knowledge of the ABC's to write a doctoral thesis! You never discard the basics; you must go on in Christ *"from glory to glory."*[8]

John's first epistle gives us another simple but profound secret of unloading that is the key to keeping the world out of your life: "Do not love the world or the things in the world. If anyone loves the world, the love of the Father is not in him" (1 Jn. 2:15).

Love Not the World So God's Light Will Shine Bright

We have to continually unload our love *of the world* to manifest the Father's love *to the world.* This too is a continuous process because we are continually bombarded by the world's temptations, attractions, and distractions. Love not the world so God's light in your life will shine bright and guide the lost back home. Too often we say we love God, but we prove by our choices that we love ourselves or the world even more. Set your priorities, and let them reflect Him as the first love and top priority in your life.

Don't be surprised if God allows a little crisis situation to challenge you from time to time to help you maintain a healthy level of dependence on Him. After all, He gave the children of Israel fresh manna every day, but made sure it would spoil if kept for more than one day. The point behind this wilderness object lesson was that God did not want His people to ever be more than 24 hours away from proving His promises are true.

Unload your burdens and ensnaring weights upon Him. Share your crisis with the Almighty God for He is able to sustain and preserve you. If you don't learn to unload crisis situations and recurring problems on Him, your mind and heart will grow weary and you will soon stumble.

Finally, keep this fact in mind: Sometimes we have to unload and turn loose of something before God can *give us something better and greater.* The Bible says, "And we know that all things work together for good to those who love God, to those who are the called according to His purpose" (Rom. 8:28). The first half of the verse comes easy, but we need to pay equal attention to the second half and remember it is *our* calling, but *His* purpose.

Are you ready and willing to unload? Don't be like some people who have such a tight claim on their problems that they wouldn't take a million dollars for them. Their conversations are peppered with possessive statements like, "*My* heart problem..." and "*My* problems with my children..." Why claim the problems? All that whining only lets the devil know you are in his neighborhood.

Even Jesus had to unload the weight of the cross temporarily. Simon carried the cross of Christ for a distance. If He couldn't reach the destination of His destiny without unloading, neither can you! He unloaded in order to reload and finish the course. Don't let present pressures postpone future destiny. There is power in proper unloading!

The 120 people who gathered together in the Upper Room in Acts chapter 1 had a lot of things to unload, and it seems that Jesus knew that. He specifically said, "Behold, I send the Promise of My Father upon you; but tarry in the city of Jerusalem until you are endued with power from on high" (Lk. 24:49). The Greek word translated as *tarry* means to "sit down, settle, and continue."[9]

What exactly did those people do in the Upper Room? They waited on the Lord and they *unloaded* every preconceived notion of what they thought God was going to do. They put aside every offense that could separate them and destroy their unity. The seven to ten days the 120 spent unloading in prayer and fasting was followed *by an instantaneous in-filling* of the Holy Spirit! It is time for us to visit the Upper Room again. We need to unload every weight and encumbrance so He can "on-load" His Spirit in power and glory!

Endnotes

1. The "burden" of the Lord can be a divine assignment for us to accomplish, a spiritual weight we are to bear in prayer until it is accomplished (Daniel bore the burden of his nation on his heart and prayed until he heard a word from God), or simply a trial or test we must go through to prepare us for another day.

2. See Heb. 12:1.

3. See Mt. 14:23, Mk. 6:31-32, 6:47; Lk. 9:18, and Jn. 6:15.

4. See Is. 9:6.

5. See Mt. 11:29-30.

6. See Mt. 14:28-30.

7. See Mt. 5:25a.

8. See 2 Cor. 3:18.

9. James Strong, *Strong's Exhaustive Concordance of the Bible* (Peabody, Massachusetts: Hendrickson Publishers, n.d.), meanings and definitions drawn from the word derivations for **tarry** (Greek, #2523, 2516).

Part II

The Power of Forgiveness

Forgiveness may be unnecessary among perfect beings, but it is vital to those of us with enough wisdom to admit we are imperfect. It seems we can't help but offend, betray, or commit wrongs against God and one another—even on our "good days" when we have the best of intentions.

Above all, we need forgiveness from our Creator just to be reconciled with Him. Once we are reconciled to God, He tells us in parable and command to extend the same forgiveness to others that He extends to us. It is a difficult assignment for such imperfect people, but there is a secret source of power in forgiveness for those with eyes to see and a will to obey.

Chapter 3

Forgiveness From the Cross to the Lost

Then Jesus said, "Father, forgive them, for they do not know what they do" (Luke 23:34a).

We are in the grip of a terminal disease for which there is no cure except God's miracle elixir of divine forgiveness. It is called sin. Forgiveness is an essential grace of God. It is one of the vital components of salvation. Without forgiveness, there is no hope for *any* of us.

Once we receive God's costly potion from the cross, it should remain in our blood, our hearts, and our way of life. For this reason, forgiveness is one of the "fruits" providing proof that Christians are changed people.

If all of this is new to you, a world of wonder awaits you. If you have "been in the way of Christ" for a number of years, you probably have a basic understanding of forgiveness. Perhaps those of us whose basic understanding has produced a measure of overconfidence about the subject of forgiveness should get "out of the way" so we can finally begin to comprehend the tremendous power of forgiveness.

In one sense, it was an "ignorant" crowd that gathered around the cross the day Jesus lifted His bloody head to pray. They were ignorant in comparison to us because we know so much more about Him now than they did then. The crowd probably didn't realize that when Jesus said, "Forgive," a tremendous release of energy and power permeated the universe and funneled down to earth. Grace was released to do its mediatorial work in that instant.

Jesus our Lord was suffering excruciating agony on the cross at Calvary when He looked toward Heaven and said, "Father, forgive them, for they do not know what they do" (Lk. 23:34a) Perhaps we should be praying, "Father, forgive us, for we know exactly what we are doing, and we are doing it anyway." Unlike the crowd gathered around the cross, we can't plead, "Guilty by ignorance."

Forgiveness Exploded Two Directions on the Human Timeline

Thank God that Jesus was not merely speaking to the profane and the perplexed who gathered around the cross two thousand years ago. Those few words from the Savior's mouth exploded in "both directions" on the timeline of human existence.

The forgiveness offered by God's Son carried the potential to forgive and cover the sins of every human being who lived in the ages prior to His brutal death on the cross at Calvary. It also carried forward in time from the bloody Mount outside Jerusalem to forgive and cover all the sins of man until His victorious second coming as Lord of lords and King of kings. The only catch to the miracle is that each person must admit their *need* for forgiveness, and choose to *receive* it from Christ Jesus as their Lord and Savior.

The power of forgiveness cannot be forced upon the unwilling, nor can it be forced by human effort or diligence to flower in barren human hearts. True forgiveness is a product of Heaven alone. It unfolds in human experience through our impossibly diverse climates like the petals of a flower. To learn its lesson, we must find the perfect bloom at the cross of Calvary. It is the summit of the world's highest hopes and the abyss of the world's deepest sorrow.

THE SWEETEST STORY OF GOD IS THE STORY OF OUR LORD'S VICTORY ON CALVARY'S BITTER CROSS.

The cross marks the place where God, robed in a regalia of battered but sinless human flesh and the bloodied garments of the condemned, courted and won our love with His life's blood. It is the place where divine power withheld its might while grace worked its greatest miracle. The sweetest story of God is the story of our Lord's victory on Calvary's bitter cross. It is God's "Ph.D. dissertation" and magnum opus on the immeasurable power of forgiveness.

When Jesus said, "*Forgive...*," the hordes of hell were bound, and satan felt the first chill signaling his miserable defeat. Within three hours, the suffering was complete and the Lord Jesus announced to the Father that His job was done.[1] Unseen hands grasped the heavy woven veil separating worshipers from the Holy of Holies in the temple and ripped it down the middle from the top to the bottom—a feat impossible for any mortal man.

Mercy danced out from the heavenly mercy seat, passed through the empty Holy of Holies[2] and the rent veil of Herod's temple to skip and twirl down the streets of Jerusalem and touch a repentant thief on one side of Jesus. Then she reached down to transform the heart of the centurion directing the Roman soldiers at the foot of the cross. She continued her dance of joy to Jerusalem's silent graveyards to kick open several tombs so certain departed saints could enjoy an early resurrection and revisit their shocked loved ones in the city.[3]

Finally, Mercy dove into hell and wrestled the keys from the devil himself and came out triumphantly shouting, "I am He who lives, and was dead, and behold, I am alive forevermore" (Rev. 1:18a). Then Jesus led captivity captive and brought forth the keys to death, hell, and the grave.[4] Can we comprehend what *power* was released in the universe when Jesus said, "Forgive"?

We must all come into the presence of forgiveness, but why should we examine such basic truths? Because it is possible— and probable—that many of the people in church congregations around the world enjoy the "culture" of church without being *changed* by an experience with God. Nothing we can say or write can typify or describe the transforming, cleansing power of God; the only way to experience it is by receiving God's forgiveness and then giving it to others. It is there, in God's forgiveness, that we find the power of a new life, the power of new hope, and the power of new joy.

Jesus Affected Three Worlds When He Said, "Forgive"

When Jesus prayed, "Father, forgive them," His words reached back in time to enfold the entire history of man before the Lord's incarnation. They covered the "present world" of His day, and reached ahead to the world that would exist after His return to Heaven. Now two thousand years or more after Jesus uttered those words, we are covered with divine forgiveness and pardon.

The day God forgave, flesh was affected, angels were affected, hell was affected, demons were affected, and the devil himself was bound. No matter how bad your life has been, the river of God's forgiveness will flow again into the cold, bitter, and hardened valleys of your heart when you come into the presence of forgiveness.

When forgiveness is present, the enemy of your soul has to back up without a word being said to him. His hands are tied and he cannot work in the presence of forgiveness. *Forgiveness puts the handcuffs of Heaven on hell itself.*

Have you ever heard someone ask, "How can I forgive someone who doesn't ask for that forgiveness?" The answer should be: "Ask Jesus." Show me one man or woman kneeling at the cross of Calvary and looking up into the face of the dying Savior to say, "Forgive us." According to the Bible's scores of eyewitnesses, no one was asking Jesus for forgiveness that day. It just didn't happen. He said, "Forgive them..." *anyway*.

THE CROSS SHOULD ALWAYS REMIND US THAT FORGIVENESS IS NOT CHEAP.

No one asked for it. No one negotiated for it. The battle-hardened Roman soldiers driving the nails, and the hard-hearted religious hypocrites who put the Lord into their hands for execution, could have cared less at the moment whether He forgave them or not. The word *forgiveness* didn't come up in the usual chatter at crucifixion time.

Forgiveness Is Not a Gimmick to Give Us Goose Bumps

The cross should always remind us that forgiveness is not cheap. What Jesus gives you is not a gimmick to give you goose bumps. It is not the product of a pep rally, or some seminar-induced positive mental attitude that you can prime like some moral pump. The kind of forgiveness Jesus brings to our lives triggers radical reconstruction of the human heart! When forgiveness is released, there is incredible power. The hand of God shattered the boundaries in every known dimension through the power of release *when Jesus forgave.*

Every one of us must deal with certain circumstances in life that cannot be changed. Perhaps Peter the fisherman wished that he could have borrowed the classic education Paul received at the feet of the renowned Jewish teacher, Gamaliel, but he would always remain Peter from Galilee. For centuries, Christians have remembered Peter as the "man who was unlearned," but who astounded the teachers of the Law who "took note that he had been with Jesus."[5]

Jesus transformed the life of Mary Magdalene the prostitute, but she still probably wished that she could undo the mistakes and pain of her past. She couldn't. Mary faced the same choice we all face: She could remain a slave to unforgiveness by clinging to her anger and resentment toward the men who abused her and the people who rejected her; or she could accept God's forgiveness, choose to forgive, and begin a life of freedom. We know the choice Mary made. What about you?

She Never Learned the Power of Forgiveness

There was a woman one time who struggled with one teacher after another throughout her life. This went on from elementary school to junior high, and from senior high through college. She had a bad experience in her early years at school with a teacher whom she was never able to forgive or forget. She carried that weight with her into her adult life. It bled over into her relationship with other role models as well and tainted her relationships at school and out of school as well. She had never learned the power of forgiveness.

There are a lot of problems in the religious world today. There are preachers who have made mistakes and a headline-hungry news media that has made sure we hear all about them. They don't tell you much at all about the other 99 percent who are men and women of the Spirit, doing the work of God in God's way every day. They just tell us about the ones who fail. You can be and probably will be disappointed by a ministry or a man of the cloth. Disappointment with one leader can rob you of relationships with others. What do you do? Forgive. You cannot live under the bondage of disappointment for your entire life. Forgive and release power.

A pastor friend was counseling a woman trying to recover from a bad marriage that had ended in divorce. Her husband had been physically and mentally abusive, eventually abandoning her and her children. It was a terrible situation. Yet, very wisely, the pastor told her that she had to let go of it. She needed to forgive her former husband for what he had done. Her response was, "He doesn't deserve to be forgiven." The pastor looked at her and said, "That may well be true—*but you do.*"

Don't Rob Yourself of Forgiveness by Clinging to Unforgiveness

This pastor's answer reveals a vital scriptural principle: *You are only forgiven as you forgive others.*[6] If you cling to unforgiveness toward another person, you are robbing yourself of your own forgiveness from God. Forgiveness toward others doesn't come naturally, it comes supernaturally.

Have you ever had to "work on" having a bad spirit? If you are like every other human being on earth, it just comes naturally to your flesh. We never have to work on being resentful. Have you ever had to tell yourself, "You know, he did me wrong and I'm going to have to work up a good case of resentment against him; it may take me three or four days to get it going good, but I'm going to work up a good case of resentment and get myself a bad spirit"? No, it just doesn't happen that way.

When resentment rises up, it comes without our even thinking about it; it is virtually instant. Forgiveness, on the other hand, takes a conscious choice and effort on our part. Our job, as born-again Christians, is to work on keeping a good attitude, a sweet spirit, and a pure heart before God and other people. This is impossible unless we learn the power of forgiveness and make right choices along the way.

Many Christians deal with another problem that is described in the statement, "I just can't forgive myself for that." This is a preposterous statement once we realize what is really being said: "Jesus, what You did on Calvary is not good enough for me." Once you have confessed your sin and found Christ in the power of the Holy Spirit, you are transformed into a new creature and the "guilty you" dies. From that moment on, if you cannot forgive yourself, it is an insult to Calvary.

If *God* forgives you, who do you think you are to say you can't forgive yourself? Are you higher and mightier than God? Are you smarter than He is? That is what your words and actions imply. The Bible says, "Therefore if the Son makes you free, you shall be free indeed" (Jn. 8:36). Accept His forgiveness! Forgive yourself! If the enemy throws something back in your face, just say, "I thank God you keep reminding me of that, devil. *I've been forgiven!* Praise God!"

There Is Preservation in Forgiveness

There is a strange law in the Old Testament that few people ever study until the topic of forgiveness comes up. God delivered the "law of remission" to Israel in the Book of Deuteronomy.[7] It required Israel to proclaim a complete and generous release of Hebrew debtors, servants, and indentured slaves every seventh year—even if they had been in bondage for only a year or less. Those in bondage had to be released and their debt or service as a slave remitted whether they had paid back their debt or not. Not only were they to be released, but their owners could not send them away empty-handed. They had to generously provide for them from their flocks, granaries, and food supplies.

This is the kind of power released by a simple act of forgiveness. It was God's way of *preserving* the life and hope of those in bondage in the Old Testament. Today we have the finished work of the cross and the shed blood of Jesus, our Redeemer. This is how the spirit of Heaven uses the power of forgiveness to remove the hiding place of demonic activity from the caverns of the human soul. Where forgiveness flourishes, resentment is removed. Where forgiveness is rare, resentment and hatred thrive.

There is power in forgiveness. Do you remember Jesus' parable about the man who owed his king ten thousand talents?[8] Scholars place widely varying values on this amount, but all of them agree it was an impossibly high amount for any employee to ever pay back.[9] If we take a middle-of-the-road estimate, then this servant owed his king ten million dollars. His monthly income plus "bonuses" probably couldn't have even paid the monthly interest on such a sum.

You Could Never Repay Me, But You Are Forgiven

When the king ordered that the man and his family members be sold to recover the debt, the man begged him, *"Forgive me! I'll repay you someday."* The king said, *"No. You'll never be able to repay me. I'll forgive the whole debt. You are forgiven."* Can you imagine how happy that man must have been? His ten-million-dollar debt had been *forgiven* and marked "Paid in Full"!

This happy man had also been owed some money, so he decided to seek out a fellow servant who owed him "a hundred pence" or only 20 dollars. Evidently, he had "loaned" the second man money from the same fortune he borrowed from the king. After being forgiven for a ten-million-dollar debt, surely this man went to tell the good news to his debtor and forgive his tiny debt as well...or did he? The Bible says, "He laid hands on him and took him by the throat, saying, 'Pay me what you owe!' " (Mt. 18:28b)

This man who had been forgiven for a multi-million-dollar debt showed no mercy to the man who owed him only 20 dollars; instead he had him thrown into jail until he could repay his debt. Our sins always find us out. The man's fellow servants were so angry when they saw what he did that they told the king. The king canceled the man's pardon and placed him in the hands of tormentors or torturers until he repaid his debt. Jesus bluntly warned His listeners then and now: "So My heavenly Father also will do to you if each of you, from his heart, does not forgive his brother his trespasses" (Mt. 18:35).

If you have that kind of spirit, cancel it. The only money the unmerciful servant had available to loan to his victim was the money loaned to him by the king! He should have offered his debtor some of the forgiveness he had received from the king. The only forgiveness we have to give is what we receive from God. We aren't any different from the servant who owed an unpayable debt: The Lord has forgiven each of us of a "multi-million-dollar debt." Don't you think we should be quick to forgive our brother or sister of their "20-dollar debt" to us? (We can't afford to say, "No.")

Have You Forgiven the Circumstances You Cannot Change?

Another group of people have imprisoned themselves in a cage of their own making clinging to their anger over circumstances in their lives which they cannot change. It doesn't matter whether the anger is directed toward God, our parents, the medical community, or "fate"; when we sow unforgiveness, we will reap a harvest of grief.

Mature Christians understand that some problems in life just can't be "solved" or removed. Our task is to seek God for the grace to go on in spite of our circumstances. The apostle Paul, who authored many of the "faith" passages in the New Testament, put it this way: "Therefore take up the whole armor of

God, that you may be able to withstand in the evil day, and having done all, to stand" (Eph. 6:13).

Paul was faced with what he called "a thorn in the flesh" that just wouldn't go away. He said:

> *Concerning this thing I pleaded with the Lord three times that it might depart from me. And He said to me, "My grace is sufficient for you, for My strength is made perfect in weakness"* (2 Corinthians 12:8-9a).

We have only one choice and one declaration as followers of Christ faced with unchanging circumstances: *I forgive. Even if I am never asked, I forgive. I am not going to keep score.* We will be crossed up if we operate in anything but God's dimension of unconditional love. We must *forgive*, regardless of who is right or wrong in a situation. *We must forgive because we must have the power of God in our lives.* Jesus set the divine example for us when He prayed from the cross, "Father, forgive them, for they do not know what they do" (Lk. 23:34a).

Forgiveness Is the Spirit of Revival Itself

Why are the most persecuted countries on earth experiencing the greatest revivals? We constantly hear and read reports of great revival springing up in countries formerly in bondage under the oppressive yoke of communism. One report said the Chinese are coming to the Lord at a rate exceeding twenty thousand per day. There are an estimated 60 million Christians there, despite the persecution faced by Christians and pastors of illegal home churches.[10]

After many years of ministry in the country of Ethiopia, we can say that virtually every Spirit-filled preacher in that nation has been put in jail, beaten, or persecuted in some way. We know one church leader whose infant was thrown through the window of their church by a soldier (the child died of the injuries sustained in the fall), and that same leader's wife has been in jail as well. They continue to proclaim the gospel of Christ. In spite of such persecution, hundreds of thousands of people have come to the Lord in Ethiopia in what has to be one of the greatest hidden revival nations in the world today. Why?

The Persecuted Must Live in a Constant Spirit of Forgiveness

Christians living under constant persecution could not survive if they did not get up every morning and say, "I forgive this system. I forgive these soldiers. I forgive this government. I forgive these circumstances." They will tell you that a tremendous power surge of the Holy Spirit accompanies a spirit of forgiveness. It gives them grace to stand and win in spite of seemingly impossible circumstances.

When Jesus Christ comes into our lives, He brings divine forgiveness with Him. He equips us with the power of forgiveness, but we have to walk in a *spirit of forgiveness* if we want to walk in the *power of His might*. Remember that His supernatural mediatorial power was released into the world when He prayed, "Father forgive...."

Are you looking for hope? Are you desperately seeking the missing link that will release you? Perhaps you realize you have been held in bondage, and now you are thinking, *I have also held other people in bondage. Now the armies of the enemy are encamped around me. How can I disperse them?*

The Holy Spirit is waiting to release you, *if you will forgive.* Don't let the excuses of your flesh or your mind distract you from what is most important right now.

I've been wronged. Who hasn't?

Life's dealt me a bad hand. So what? Join the club.

I was lied to. You're not the first one. You won't be the last one. Your Master was lied to. Are you any better than He is?

Those who were supposed to have been my friends forsook me. Join the club. Jesus is president. They all forsook Him and fled.

If you need help, ask God to help you forgive and release those people or circumstances that have hurt you. Ask Him to forgive you for every sin and failure in your life. He is faithful to forgive. He says, "The one who comes to Me I will by no means cast out" (Jn. 6:37b).

You were forgiven on Calvary, if you will only appropriate God's forgiveness. Do it now and experience the sweet release that comes when the God of Heaven forgives you once and for all. Do you doubt that you are a Christian? He says to you, *"Take up My cross and follow Me."*[11] It all begins with the same first step: Experience the power of divine forgiveness.

Endnotes

1. See Lk. 23:44-47.
2. The Holy of Holies in Jerusalem's Temple of Herod was empty. The ark of the covenant and the furniture of the temples of the past had been lost long before Jesus' day.
3. See Mt. 27:52-54.
4. See Eph. 4:8.
5. See Acts 4:13.
6. See Mt. 6:14.
7. See Deut. 15:1-18.
8. See Mt. 18:23-35.
9. The "guestimates" vary from more than 30 million dollars (based on the talent as a "measure of silver alloy" common in the Old Testament) to ten million dollars (cited in The Amplified Bible), to a more conservative 3.8 million dollars (based on the "Roman-Attic talent" current under Roman occupation) cited by W.E. Vine, *Vines Expository Dictionary of Old and New Testament Words*, (Old Tappen, New Jersey: Fleming H. Revell Company, 1981), "talent," p. 108.

10. Courtesy of WorldHelp, an interdenominational Bible distribution ministry based in Forest, Virginia. WorldHelp cited these statistics on its Internet Web site, using some figures supplied by the Chinese Church Research Center (from *http://www.worldhelp.net/bibles/china.asp* on 2/28/2000).

11. See Mk 8:34.

Chapter 4

This Is Between You and Me

*For if you forgive men their trespasses, your heavenly
Father will also forgive you* (Matthew 6:14).

Wouldn't it be nice to live in *perpetual revival* and a *continuous harvest* of souls for Christ? We could and we should; but among other things, we have to learn how to live together in a spirit of forgiveness before that can happen. Forgiveness brings unity and unity helps bring revival.

The power of God is released every time we forgive one another. Individuals, families, churches, and even entire cities can experience revival when forgiveness is present. Jesus showed us that when pardon is abundantly given, a deafening and sometimes spectacular release of power comes against evil in the heavenly places. The dark principalities and powers of hell are neutralized by such an outpouring of grace. The apostle Paul, in his letter to the church at Colosse, painted a picture of the Lord's triumph of forgiveness on the cross and how it affected us:

> *And you...He has made alive together with Him, having* **forgiven you all trespasses**, *having* **wiped out the handwriting of requirements** *that was against us,*

which was contrary to us. And He has **taken it out of the way, having nailed it to the cross.** *Having* **disarmed principalities and powers,** *He* **made a public spectacle of them,** *triumphing over them in it* (Colossians 2:13-15).

Jesus' prayer, *"Father, forgive them,"* released a miracle of forgiveness that changed the course of history. There is power in forgiveness. Despite the excruciating pain Jesus felt when Roman soldiers pounded large iron spikes through His hands and feet, He was thinking of forgiveness. When death finally came, forgiveness was ours and Christ's blood had purchased our freedom for eternity.

The power of divine forgiveness crushed hell's gates, opened the cold tombs of the dead, and raised the bodies of the faithful. The heavy veil in the temple was split down the center from the top to the bottom and Heaven itself was opened by Jesus' selfless sacrifice. Again, it all happened because He prayed, *"Father, forgive them,"* and His prayer was answered.

Jesus' Prayer of Forgiveness Unleashed the Power of God

Jesus' words and deeds on the cross unleashed God's supernatural power of forgiveness and set in motion a divine sequence of events:

1. *He forgave all of our trespasses or debts.* He also taught us to pray, "Forgive us our debts, as we forgive our debtors" (Mt. 6:12). A debt is something legally owed. Perhaps someone legally and rightfully owes you an apology, but it is a debt they will not pay. What do you do? Forgive them anyway.

2. *He canceled out our decree of death* when He wiped out the laws and regulations we could never keep, and the

mountain of sins we accumulated. Then He took the whole document of rules, the list of our failures, and the certificate of death and nailed it to the cross as something to be crucified and buried. If people don't respond to your forgiveness, it becomes their problem, not yours. Offer it anyway. Sometimes you have to settle for the proverbial "fifty cents on the dollar" in matters like this. You are responsible for your half of the settlement—the *forgiving* and *canceling* part.

3. *He disarmed the principalities and powers* when He forgave our debts and sins. Forgiveness tore up hell's playground, and your forgiveness of others destroys the best-laid plans of the enemy meant for their destruction.

Do you want God's power in your life? It comes with the power of forgiveness. *When you forgive you cancel the debt and evict the devil.* How can we make the claim this "evicts the devil"? We aren't claiming the enemy can "have" you, but the Bible makes it clear there are ways he can legally claim the right to "hitch a ride" and harass you if there is resentment or unforgiveness in your life.

Jesus said in one place, *"The ruler of this world is coming, and he has nothing in Me"* (Jn. 14:30b). Satan lives in darkness and he cannot bear the light of God's glory. He persistently works to get one little shaft of darkness into your heart in the form of resentment, unforgiveness, or a spirit of bitterness toward someone else. The apostle Paul said,

"Be angry, and do not sin": do not let the sun go down on your wrath, **nor give place to the devil** (Ephesians 4:26-27).

Now whom you forgive anything, I also forgive. For if indeed I have forgiven anything, I have forgiven that one for your sakes in the presence of Christ, **lest satan**

should take advantage of us; for we are not igno-rant of his devices (2 Corinthians 2:10-11).

Unforgiveness in any form gives satan a comfortable "place" of darkness that becomes a legal handle or handgrip on your life from which he can take advantage of you and make your life miserable. (The darkness of sin doesn't belong to God; it is part of satan's realm. It gives satan "stock" in your life, so he can rightfully show up at your "stockholder meetings" and wreak havoc.) However, the enemy lives in darkness. As long as you are full of the light of God's presence without the darkness of unforgiveness, that light has the power to totally dispel and repel satan from every area of your life.

Any discussion concerning the devil and his kingdom should be conducted from the perspective of our new position in Christ. In the Book of Ephesians, we are told that God *"raised us up together, and made us sit together in the heavenly places in Christ Jesus"* (Eph. 2:6).

The devil's principalities and powers are not "looking down on us"; we are looking down on them from our spiritual position in Christ, seated in heavenly places. The forces of darkness are *beneath* us because they are bound by the power of the blood of the Lamb, the name of Jesus, the Word of God, and the power of forgiveness.

We Are Obligated to Forgive—Whether They Deserve It or Not

Forgiveness is God's tool of freedom and power in your hand when you feel emotionally strapped and trapped by circumstances or the wrongdoings of others. God inspired us with His love and Jesus gave us the supreme example of forgiveness on the cross. Now we are obligated to our Lord to extend the power of forgiveness toward others—whether they deserve it or not. This is the way *obligation follows inspiration.*

Just as Jesus' forgiveness disarmed the devil on a cosmic scale, so will our pardon of others in this life disarm the enemy in earthly relationships. Think of the last time you forgave someone: Can you remember the tremendous release you felt at that moment?

Do you know Christians who wonder why they feel "bound" or weighted down? They often say they can't get any release in their experience with God or make any spiritual progress. Perhaps these saints are harboring small pockets of resentment in their hearts. (It is easy to do and hard to admit.) The key to victory is only a decision away. They need to forgive and release others so the power of forgiveness can be released in their own lives.

FORGIVENESS IS ONE OF THE LEAST-KNOWN SECRETS OF ANSWERED PRAYER.

Forgiveness is one of the least-known secrets of answered prayer. It is a vital key to exercising power over principalities and powers. We have no choice as followers of Christ: We must live in a spirit of forgiveness. Two brothers discovered this secret long ago. Isaac's twin sons, Esau and Jacob, were as different as two brothers could be. Jacob cheated his older brother, Esau, of two of life's most valuable things in Bible times—the elder son's birthright as head of the family and inheritor of the family fortune after his father's death, and the father's special blessing reserved for the eldest son.

The only thing that kept Jehovah from being known as "the God of Abraham, Isaac, and Esau" was one bowl of soup. Esau played his part in the tragedy by yielding to his fleshly desires instead of valuing the truly valuable, but there is no doubt that Jacob cheated Esau. There is even less doubt that Jacob deceived his father and cheated Esau again by stealing his blessing from Isaac. There was fire in Esau's eyes and Jacob fled for his life. Years later, Esau came after Jacob with four hundred men and Jacob had run out of places to hide—except for one. He had a life-changing encounter with God and discovered the power of forgiveness.

The Power of Forgiveness Caused Esau to Run to Jacob in Tears

When Jacob finally met Esau and his band of men, he humbled himself and bowed to the ground seven times before his brother, *seeking genuine forgiveness and reconciliation.* There was something different about Jacob and Esau recognized it. The forgiveness flowing from God through Jacob literally flooded Esau's embittered heart and instantly transformed him. The Bible says that Esau *ran* to meet his brother, and embraced him in tears.[1] Only God's power of forgiveness can release this kind of power to transform a person's life.

In a matter of seconds, forgiveness washed away 27 years of simmering bitterness and hatred! There was no doubt that Esau had been wronged or that Jacob was a deceiver and a master con-artist. Yet when Jacob released forgiveness from his own heart, Heaven flooded Esau's life. His weeping washed the bitterness away. Jacob's three bands of men could not stop Esau, nor could Jacob's gifts of wealth. In the end, only forgiveness could stop Esau and end their lifelong feud.

Are there things harbored in your heart against someone that you have simply chosen not to forgive? It is a dangerous thing. Your failure to forgive others prevents God's ability to forgive you. Bitter or better—it's your choice!

Forgiveness Is More Important for Us Than for "Them"

We need to forgive whether we feel we have a "right" to be angry or not. It is actually more important for us than it is for "them" because forgiveness keeps our hearts "clean" and it pleases God. If anyone in the Old Testament had a "right" to be angry with other people, it was Joseph. His jealous older brothers plotted to kill him, but decided to sell him into slavery instead. He worked as a slave to Pharaoh's head guard in Egypt, then he ended up in Pharaoh's prison after being falsely accused. Joseph refused to dwell on his "rights" or his "wrongs," and instead chose to forgive. This qualified him for God's favor and blessing and he was elevated to the number two position in Egypt as ruler under Pharaoh at the age of 30.

When Joseph finally met his brothers again, he had every "right" to be bitter and resentful (if there is such a thing). They had mistreated him and deceived their father, and Joseph had the power to order them killed on the spot. Instead, Joseph *chose* to forgive them and he became a savior to his entire family. When he saw his brothers, he couldn't control himself. He wept so loudly that the whole household of Pharaoh heard him. The world needs to know that "the community of the changed" know how to forgive. The lost and hurting around us need to know there is abundant forgiveness in the house and family of God.

God intends for our forgiveness to literally preserve and protect the lives of those who misuse or abuse us until they can turn their hearts to Him. Joseph's brothers were overcome with guilt and he begged them to forgive themselves. He said:

> *But now, do not therefore be grieved or angry with yourselves because you sold me here; for God sent me before you to preserve life....And God sent me before you to preserve a posterity for you in the earth, and to save your lives by a great deliverance* (Genesis 45:5,7).

This is the character of God! It is higher than any "right" we could ever have. Joseph never gave any evidence that he was bitter over his mistreatment by his brothers. He lived *a lifestyle of forgiveness.*

We Must Release Any "Prisoners" in Our Heart

Sometimes we think we have forgiven someone when the truth is that we have reserved a special little room, a hidden closet of bitterness, buried deep in our heart that we hope God never visits. We keep the person who offended us locked up in that secret place. When we are alone, we indulge ourselves by remembering "what they did to us ten years ago." Then we mentally pull out the offender and "beat up on them" for a while.

We like to say, "Oh, that's under the blood," but it isn't. The devil likes to hide in our secret rooms inhabited by an unforgiving spirit, but no devil or demon in hell can withstand forgiveness. The "prisoner" in our hearts has to be released. We must forgive and release the power of God in our lives.

The people of Jerusalem played the game of "now you are forgiven, now you are not" with disastrous results during the life and ministry of Jeremiah the prophet. King Zedekiah had imprisoned Jeremiah for prophesying the fall of Jerusalem to Babylon when they were surrounded by the armies of King Nebuchadnezzar of Babylon and his allies. They faced impossible odds with no way of escape, but God had a plan that still applies to His people today.

After Jeremiah prophesied to King Zedekiah that the city would fall but he would live, the king decided to observe the "law of remission" (described in the previous chapter). He called together the people of Jerusalem and they made a covenant to free all of their fellow Jews who were bond servants in their homes. They forgave every debt owed by their brethren and set them free, even though the debts weren't fully paid.

Forgive and Flood the Enemy's Camp With God's Power

The king of Babylon and his armies withdrew from the city when the people of Jerusalem showed mercy and extended forgiveness toward one another.[2] It appears their forgiveness on earth actually bound the purposes of satan in the heavenlies! When we start forgiving one another, God floods the enemy's camp with His power.

God gave the people of Judah and Jerusalem a final opportunity to "get right" with Him and "do right" to one another. If they had seized it, then the Book of Lamentations would have never been written. Sadly, once the Babylonians left, the people of Jerusalem did something terrible. When they were under the fear of death, they released their slaves, but when the fear of death was removed, they returned to their selfishness, *and God noted it.* They put their brothers right back into slavery, prompting this reply from God:

> *Thus says the Lord, the God of Israel: "I made a covenant with your fathers in the day that I brought them out of the land of Egypt, out of the house of bondage, saying, 'At the end of seven years let every man set free his Hebrew brother, who has been sold to him; and when he has served you six years, you shall let him go free from you.'* **But your fathers did not obey Me nor incline their ear.** *Then* **you recently turned and did what was right in My sight;** *every man proclaiming liberty to his neighbor; and you made a covenant before Me in the house which is called by My name.* **Then you turned around and profaned My name, and every one of you brought back his male and female slaves, whom he had set at liberty,** *at their pleasure, and* **brought them back into subjection,** *to be your male and female slaves." Therefore thus says the Lord: "You have not obeyed Me in proclaiming liberty, every one to his brother and every one to his neighbor. Behold, I proclaim liberty to you," says the Lord; "to the sword, to pestilence, and to famine! And I will deliver you to trouble among all the kingdoms of the earth"* (Jeremiah 34:13-17).

Don't Dig Up Old Offenses—Release Your Debtors Forever

When the people of Jerusalem re-enslaved their brethren and canceled their forgiveness, the armies of Nebuchadnezzar came back and gave them exactly what they had given each other. The former "owners" were carried off to Babylon as slaves while their former slaves remained behind to take possession of their land and belongings. How many times have we forgiven a brother or sister in Christ only to go "dig up" their offense again and place them back into the slavery of our unforgiveness? God *still* notes it.

Are you prepared if God suddenly calls for an "audit" of your conduct toward your brothers and sisters? Remember that He doesn't need an audit—He already sees and knows all things. He holds each of us personally responsible for forgiving others, with no exceptions to the rule. We were not created or designed to carry bitterness and unforgiveness in our hearts. It is like trying to carry battery acid in a Styrofoam cup—the acid of unforgiveness eats away at every part of our lives.

Jesus said His disciples would be known for their love for one another.[3] Love transcends the "ledger-sheet mentality" that keeps track of every wrong done and offense received. The "God-kind-of-love" described in First Corinthians chapter 13 doesn't keep a score or an "account" of wrongs suffered.[4]

"Mercy [always] triumphs over judgment" (Jas. 2:13b), so operate in love and "set your slaves free." Release the power of forgiveness in your life. God is saying, "If you show mercy to others, I will show you mercy."

We also need to learn how to *forgive ourselves*. It is difficult to keep Jesus' command to "love others as we love ourselves" when we really don't love ourselves. Many times, self-hatred or inner resentments build up because of our fear of failure or rejection.

Practice the Three Keys of Forgiveness

One of the greatest mistakes we can make in life is to live in constant fear that we will make a mistake. Mark Twain said that if a cat sits on a hot stove, he will never do it again. *Of course, he won't sit on a cold stove either.* Failure has a tendency to make us quit trying. If you have been knocked down a few times or have experienced some setbacks, *don't quit!* Learn the power of forgiveness. *Forgive yourself and get back up again.* Practice the three keys of forgiveness:

- Forgive circumstances.

- Forgive people.

- Forgive yourself.

Just forgive so God's power can be released in your life. It will bring strength to help you stand up again after a hard fall, to press forward and strive for success even in the fading light of yesterday's failure.

Successful people usually fail more often than others do; they succeed primarily because they just won't quit trying. It is certain that any person who has been successful is also a person who has failed. Just as a baby can't learn how to walk without falling down a few times, you can't make progress in life without stumbling a few times along the way. In American football, the man who gets knocked down the most is usually the one who carries the ball most often and gains the most yardage for his team.

Forgiveness operates under the divine law of "sowing and reaping." The New Testament says, "Do not be deceived, God is not mocked; for whatever a man sows, that he will also reap" (Gal. 6:7). Sow forgiveness today for a harvest of mercy and forgiveness tomorrow and in the years to come. Don't let unforgiveness take over your home, your marriage, or your business. A spirit of unforgiveness does not make for a happy ending. Weep, repent, and forgive so the strongholds of hell in your life will be torn down. Our lives will be flooded with power if we can only forgive.

Forgive, and avoid getting caught up in the "numbers" of forgiveness like Peter did. He asked Jesus:

Then Peter came to Him and said, "Lord, how often shall my brother sin against me, and I forgive him? Up to seven times?" Jesus said to him, "I do not say to you, up to seven times, but up to seventy times seven" (Matthew 18:21-22).

Jesus basically said, *"No, Peter, you have missed the spirit behind the forgiveness. You have a 'calculator heart.' Don't try to put a measuring stick on forgiveness and on God. You are to forgive them seventy-times-seven times if necessary."* Jesus kept "raising the bar" on forgiveness until no one could reach the limit. To forgive someone 490 times during a 16-hour day, you would have to forgive them for the same offense 30 times an hour or *once every two minutes.* Forgiveness is a full-time job! Forgiveness is a lifestyle. Don't try to keep score.

God is adamant when He tells us repeatedly in His Word to *forgive* others. Do you want to live in freedom and victory?

Forgive.

Forgive.

Forgive.

(And keep on forgiving.)

Endnotes

1. See Gen. 33:4.
2. See Jer. 34:21-22.
3. See Jn. 13:35.
4. See 1 Cor. 13:5. The *New International Version* says love "keeps no record of wrongs."

Part III

The Power Behind the Throne

*Son of man, take up a lamentation for the king of Tyre,
and say to him, "Thus says the Lord God: 'You were the
seal of perfection, full of wisdom and perfect in beauty.
You were in Eden, the garden of God; every precious
stone was your covering: the sardius, topaz, and dia-
mond, beryl, onyx, and jasper, sapphire, turquoise, and
emerald with gold. The workmanship of your timbrels
and pipes was prepared for you on the day you were created. You were the anointed cherub who covers; I established you; you were on the holy mountain of God; you
walked back and forth in the midst of fiery stones. You
were perfect in your ways from the day you were created,
till iniquity was found in you. By the abundance of your
trading you became filled with violence within, and you
sinned; therefore I cast you as a profane thing out of the
mountain of God; and I destroyed you, O covering
cherub, from the midst of the fiery stones. Your heart was
lifted up because of your beauty; you corrupted your wisdom for the sake of your splendor; I cast you to the
ground, I laid you before kings, that they might gaze at
you. You defiled your sanctuaries by the multitude of*

your iniquities, by the iniquity of your trading; therefore I brought fire from your midst; it devoured you, and I turned you to ashes upon the earth in the sight of all who saw you. All who knew you among the peoples are astonished at you; you have become a horror, and shall be no more forever' " (Ezekiel 28:12-19).

Chapter 5

The Power Behind the Throne

Nations at war expend great amounts of money and resources on military intelligence to learn everything possible about their enemies. The Church and the Kingdom of God are at war with satan and his dark kingdom in a limited sense. It is limited because we battle a "defeated foe" whose sentence has already been decreed and his final day of freedom has been determined by God.

We have no need to build a military intelligence operation because God already knows everything about the archangel He created who was formerly called "Lucifer, son of the morning."[1] We often hear the phrase, "Knowledge is power," and there is truth in those words. God's Word contains vital information and knowledge about the devil and his ways. We need that knowledge to effectively overcome his hindering schemes in the earth.

Admittedly, the devil isn't worthy of as much focus and attention some give him, but we do need to know how to stop his hindering ways while we are pursuing God's purposes. This knowledge is one of the secret sources of power God has given to us. The apostle Paul demonstrated this in the Book of Acts. He put up with the antics of a spirit of divination as long as he could, but finally he had to stop and expose the demonic spirit for what it was and cast it out of the woman who had followed him for several days.[2]

The devil's greatest weapon is deception, and he uses it skillfully against those who are unaware or unprepared for his assault. It is for this reason that Paul wrote to the Corinthians:

Now whom you forgive anything, I also forgive. For if indeed I have forgiven anything, I have forgiven that one for your sakes in the presence of Christ, lest satan should take advantage of us; for we are not ignorant of his devices (2 Corinthians 2:10-11).

Someone once said, "Behind every successful man stands a supportive wife—and a surprised mother-in-law." This humorous remark has a measure of truth in it. Have you ever heard the phrase, "The power behind the throne"?

He Spoke Directly to the Power Behind the Throne

Ezekiel the prophet delivered a stinging prophecy from God for someone called "the Prince of Tyre" and later on "the King of Tyre." This same king was addressed in earlier chapters, but 11 verses into chapter 28, God seemed to interrupt the prophet and he suddenly changed the tone of the message. It is as if he *looked beyond the throne of the earthly king* to address the hidden power that was actually motivating and directing his actions. God wanted him to speak directly to the *power **behind** the throne*:

Son of man, take up a lamentation for the king of Tyre, and say to him, "Thus says the Lord God: 'You were the seal of perfection, full of wisdom and perfect in beauty. You were in Eden, the garden of God....You were the anointed cherub who covers; I established you; you were on the holy mountain of God; you walked back and forth in the midst of fiery stones. You were perfect in your ways from the day you were created...'" (Ezekiel 28:12-15).

Ezekiel the prophet was not saying these things to the man sitting on the earthly throne of Tyre; he was looking beyond him to address satan, the fallen angel who was once called Lucifer, the anointed cherub who covers. This exiled cherub of rebellion was *the real power behind the throne.*

Lucifer was anointed to worship, and he exercised some level of dominion over economy and commerce (which should tell us that wealth is not always indicative of God's power).

One Power Manipulated the Figurehead of Flesh

There was a literal king of Tyre, and he was a wicked man known for his fierce pride and cruelty. His deeds earned him God's wrath, and the Lord pronounced woes and curses upon him. However, in verse 11, the Lord shifted His attention beyond the figurehead of flesh to address the proud spirit hidden behind the throne. He spoke directly to Lucifer/satan, the power who was manipulating and operating the earthly king's life, and predicted his outcome and foretold his downfall.

Adolph Hitler ascended to power in Germany in the 1930s and successfully engineered the murder of millions of Jews in his attempt to take over the world in World War II. Others like him rose up in the years that followed. Millions of alleged "enemies of the state" were secretly "liquidated" in Russia at the personal command of the Soviet leader, Joseph Stalin. More recently, in the African nation of Uganda, General Idi Amin overthrew the president of his nation and launched an eight-year reign of terror. He slaughtered three hundred thousand of his fellow Ugandans before an invasion force from Tanzania forced him to flee the country in 1979. Saddam Hussein became president of Iraq that same year, and managed to murder even more of his people using illegal biochemical weapons that have been banned by every civilized nation in the world.

Each of these men did incredibly wicked things that brought darkness to entire generations, but those who could look "behind the throne" had no doubts about the true power behind all the death and destruction. These men will be held responsible for their deeds before the Almighty God, but the true power motivating and empowering their acts of mass evil came from behind the throne. Again, the fallen archangel, satan, was doing everything he could to destroy God's highest creation and separate them from Him.

Do Your Actions Glorify What Satan Stands For?

Satan is attracted by any atmosphere that has one or more of his own characteristics. People don't realize they can easily create an atmosphere that attracts him by doing things that glorify what he stands for.

We know that we can create an atmosphere that attracts the Holy Spirit or grieves and repulses Him. God's Word tells us to, "Enter into His gates with thanksgiving, and into His courts with praise. Be thankful to Him, and bless His name" (Ps. 100:4). When we thank the Lord, praise Him, and bless His name, we find ourselves in His presence. It is a question of attitude.

What attitudes create a comfortable place for satan? We know the actions and activities of the King of Tyre created such a comfortable atmosphere for satan that he took up residence behind his throne and empowered the king to do his evil bidding.

Many of the evil things happening in our day are not merely the work of flesh and blood. Paul warned us not to fight on the "wrong front." He said, "We do not wrestle against flesh and blood, but against principalities, against powers, against the rulers of the darkness of this age, against spiritual hosts of wickedness in the heavenly places" (Eph. 6:12). We don't need to "look for a demon under every rock," but much of the evil that appears to be human activity alone is motivated, directed, and even empowered by demonic principalities, powers, and spiritual wickedness in high places.

Evil human attitudes and actions create a welcoming "comfort zone" or atmosphere where the enemy can work even greater demonic evil in comfort and concealment. An atmosphere of disunity is especially attractive to the enemy because it *empowers* him. When people get in disunity, they commit spiritual treason and their actions weaken God's Kingdom and strengthen satan's position. He constantly works to make us believe our real battle is against other people, but his favorite tactic is to pit brother against brother in the family of God. When it works, he just hides behind our thrones and laughs. His kingdom is secure for the moment because just as *unity brings revival,* so will *disunity dispel it!*

Proud and Ripe for Satanic Manipulation

The Gospels of Matthew and Mark tell us that one day Simon Peter declared Jesus' true identity as the Son of God by revelation of the Holy Spirit, and received Jesus' praise for his discernment. Then Jesus announced that He would die and rise again, and Peter rebuked Him for saying it! He said, "It will never happen to You, Lord! No, sir, we're going to stand with You...."[3] Peter's religious words sounded good. They had the ring of true devotion and sincerity, but they were diabolically wrong.

Simon Peter's pride and presumption created an atmosphere ripe for a satanic visitation. The enemy joined their dinner party and used unsuspecting Peter to proclaim the hopes of hell. Satan must have snickered when Peter told Jesus the Messiah that He was wrong to say He was going to die on the cross. The words had hardly left Peter's mouth before Jesus confronted him. Looking beyond the familiar face of Simon Peter, the Lord directly addressed the evil archangel hiding "behind the throne":

"Get behind Me, satan! You are an offense to Me, for you are not mindful of the things of God, but the things of men" (Mt. 16:23b).

There are times when "doing right" by your definition is actually "doing wrong" by God's. Something is "right" when it is lined up with God's Word and confirmed by His Spirit. Peter experienced that when he accurately declared Jesus' true identity. However, he had to completely dismiss the reality of Jesus' identity that he had just discovered in order to say what he did. If Jesus was the Son of God, why would He lie about His destiny?

When your action seems "right" but the way you go about it is wrong, it is the worst kind of "wrongness" because it can deceive and lead others down the wrong path as well. Peter was saying, "You won't die. We will stand by You," but Jesus knew He could never accomplish His purpose on earth without Calvary. Anything that could or would attempt to block the purposes of God could not be from God. *All good ideas are not "God ideas."*

Doing Right Can Be Wrong (If It Is the Wrong Time and Way)

If the enemy cannot get us to do wrong with a trap or an enticement, then he tries to trick us into "doing right" at the wrong time or in the wrong way. Few things are more damaging than someone who is absolutely sincere—and sincerely *wrong*. Always remember that the devil used to sit "at the best table in town." He still knows how to set a beautiful table and make it look perfect and enticing. He always uses things that sound so good to us that we can't believe they are not of God.

It is so easy to blame the "King of Tyre" or Peter for everything they did. However, we need to look at the real power behind the throne. The flesh wants to blame the people in the front row, but the Spirit of God sees past the "front men" and looks beyond the concealment of the throne. God knew that both of these men had been manipulated by satan for his own ends.

Paul said we are dealing with spiritual wickedness in high places, so that means that the battles we fight are not always clear-cut. We have to learn to *know* our enemy. Jesus understood that when He looked past Peter and said, "Get behind Me, satan," He wasn't calling Peter the devil. He bypassed Peter and went directly to the one who put the thought into Peter's mind.

Satan is "the accuser of the brethren." He isn't omnipresent, so he can't accuse all of us by himself. He still manages to get the same effect by "recruiting" brother to accuse brother and sister to accuse sister. He even uses our "prayers" to take his false complaints to the ears of God! How does he do it? He encourages us to "pray/complain" things like this: "Oh, Lord, do You know what Sister Sue said about me? It's a terrible thing, Lord. Please reveal to her the error of her ways."

Words That Accuse Are Not Words of Prayer

It doesn't matter whether an accusation is framed in the softening language of kindness or wrapped in religious slang—it still isn't prayer. The devil doesn't have to worry about accusing everyone as long as he can keep certain saints busy doing it for him in the name of prayer. For many of us, he doesn't even have to disguise it as prayer. He simply dials up the largest Christian communication network in the world.

You can sneeze in San Francisco and by the time the "Gossiping Saint Network" (the "GSN") relays it to Manhattan, the story has grown enough to put you on your deathbed with double-lung pneumonia! Any lack of commitment to truth on our part becomes an open invitation to the enemy to make himself comfortable in our lives.

If satan is the accuser or self-appointed prosecutor of the saints and Jesus is our advocate or defense attorney, where do we fit in? If you defend your brother, the spirit of Jesus operates through you. If you accuse your brother, whose spirit is working through you?

Who Is This Fallen Prince of Heaven and King of Hell?

We know who the King of glory is, but who is this fallen prince of Heaven and king of hell who was in the garden of Eden? The Bible says Lucifer was perfect in all his ways until "the day of iniquity."[4] *Iniquity is rebellion against divine authority.* In First Samuel 15:23a, Samuel prophesied to Saul that "...rebellion is as the sin of witchcraft, and stubbornness is as iniquity and idolatry." When a stubborn man—or angel—worships his own opinion, it becomes an idol and an enemy of God.

We know of three archangels or cherubs in the Bible. Two of these ruling angels possess great power and responsibility before God: Gabriel is God's primary messenger angel while Michael is His chief angelic warrior, commanding general of the angelic armies of Heaven, and the protector of Israel. The third archangel, Lucifer, was the covering cherub. He served as the chief worship leader and attendant to God Himself until he fell into sin. At that point, he was stripped of all heavenly authority and every trace of God's glory; and darkness gripped his very being for eternity.

The Bible tells us Lucifer was created in perfection. He was one of God's noblest creatures surpassing in beauty and wisdom. Lucifer literally means "light bearer" or "morning star." It is possible that he was created to reflect the light of God and His glory throughout the heavenly realms as he worshiped the Most High unceasingly before Adam was created.

This cherub was covered with genius and was designed with multiple voices so he could produce multiple tones like a heavenly pipe organ. His voice was unmatched in beauty and sheer power to move his hearers. (In other words, he was very persuasive.)

Pride Is the Worst of All Spiritual Cancers

All of that ended the day iniquity was found in Lucifer. The covering cherub looked away from the Almighty to lust after His position and said in his heart, "I will ascend into Heaven, I will exalt my throne above the stars of God....I will ascend above the heights of the clouds, I will be like the Most High" (Is. 14:13b-14). Lucifer's iniquity took the form of pride, the worst of all spiritual cancers. *It instantly transformed the son of morning into the son of darkness.* Pride is the worst of all sins, for it existed in Heaven even before there was "a devil."

Satan used pride to engineer the downfall of Eve in the garden of Eden, and he is still using it against God's people today. Sometimes it comes clothed in false humility, but that is just "pride with another face." (Did you hear about the man who was given a medal for being humble? He pinned it on himself and they took it away from him.)

Genuine humility is the most sensitive of graces, but pride in any form is driven to express itself. Whether it shows up as a haughty spirit or a condescending attitude, the sin of pride always leads to rebellion if there is no repentance. Lucifer's heart was lifted up and he refused to repent because he wanted to stand in the place of God. The Holy God had no choice but to instantly expel darkness from the Kingdom of light, and Lucifer became satan—the "adversary"—an exile from Heaven with no place to go but down.

Satan and his works belong to the kingdom of darkness, while the Bible says, "For you were once darkness, but now you are light in the Lord. Walk as children of light" (Eph. 5:8). We cannot support, defend, or adopt anything that is darkness. We must stay alert to the true power behind the "thrones" or flesh and blood opponents to God and His Kingdom. Whether it is politically correct or not, God expects us to call evil evil, and good good.

Don't Fight With Your Tongue, Fight on Your Knees

Whether we like the terminology or not, these are "battle tactics." The simple truth about "spiritual warfare" is that most of the battles we try to fight with our tongues are better fought on our knees. The greatest battles are waged in the heavenlies, and by definition, *spiritual warfare* is a *spiritual* thing that must be won in the *spirit realm*. As for the tongue, it is like a double-edged sword. It may not weigh much, but very few people can hold it (including most Christians). We usually end up doing more damage than good once our tongues get going.

> **SPIRITUAL WARFARE IS A SPIRITUAL THING THAT MUST BE WON IN THE SPIRIT REALM.**

Even though satan is a loser whose entire existence has been corrupted by pride, he still has enough traces of angelic beauty, light, and intelligence to transform himself into an angel of light when necessary.[5] He is both brilliantly stupid and seductively beautiful, and this combination of traits makes satan especially dangerous to the uninformed, "partially-knowledgeable" Christian. Satan still knows how angels are supposed to operate and often he can fool those who have failed to "rightly divide the word of truth."[6]

Some people wonder why satan doesn't show up more often in the Old Testament. By one count, satan or Lucifer appears only 15 times in just four of the 39 books of the Old Testament, yet the four Gospels alone mention satan, the devil, or evil spirits at least 61 times.[7] Why? When Jesus the light of the world arrived, His piercing light illuminated the darkness and exposed the old serpent for what he was. The Lord planted the Church on a hill to be the light of the world after His resurrection, and commanded us to do what He did: to expose and destroy the works of satan.

The devil can be very deceptive. We know he can *appear* to be an angel of light. It is almost guaranteed he will *not* show up in a red suit with horns and a pitchfork. It would be too easy for us to recognize him. He prefers to approach us in various disguises. Our love for "stereotypes and assumptions" about the enemy is another weakness he uses against us.

Some Folks Have "Just the Right Atmosphere" for Satan

Many Christians are fooled when they assume satan only shows up in seedy bars, crack shacks, or houses of ill repute. Actually, he already "owns" those places, so they don't require his personal attention. He is more likely to be often found hiding behind the pews in God's house near folks who have "just the right atmosphere" of rebellion, jealousy, resentment, or unforgiveness in their hearts. He doesn't own that house yet, but he has been after the property since time began.

Satan has a special ability to infiltrate areas of beauty and creativity such as the visual arts, music, and literature. Satan is not creative because he lost all creativity the day his relationship with the God of creation (and creativity) was severed. However, he can still recognize creativity in the human race, and *he is quick to add demonic power to human ability*—for the price of a soul and the right to corrupt it for his purposes. That is why some of the material labeled as "quality literature" today is nothing more than X-rated pornographic reading.

The enemy is just clever enough to help gullible humans phrase their twisted thoughts to fit the minimum criteria for "art." He knows how to mix sensuous body language, alluring beat, and X-rated lyrics to entice the human heart and win every award the world has to offer! It is sad but true: We are easily lured by the beauty and deceived by the power behind the throne.

"The Devil Fell Into My Choir!"

Where does satan concentrate his efforts the most? If you ask any seasoned church leader, it is almost certain they will tell you "the church music department." Satan hates the anointing God places on music and worship more than any other. It is alleged that Martin Luther, the cleric who sparked the Reformation, said, "When the devil fell out of Heaven, he fell in my choir"! Satan targets music and worship above everything else because it used to be *his anointing.* He can't stand the thought that the ministry and anointing he forfeited through rebellion has been given to us! Let us fix this fact about anointed music and worship in our hearts and minds: Satan hates it, despises it, and seeks to destroy it at all costs.

It is understandable that satan hates the worship anointing, but what is all the fuss? He can't stop the worship in Heaven, can he? All of us have heard people talk or even preach about angels singing in Heaven, but what do the Scriptures say? They tell us the angels sang at creation, and they predict prophetically that angels will sing in the eternity to come after the saints join them around the throne. However, there is *no Bible record* of angels singing between those two times!

Scores of uplifting Christmas carols and classical works spring to mind to deny that statement; however, we should closely examine the Scriptures describing the Advent or birth of Christ. Look at the most popular Christmas *doxa* or praise passage of all in Luke's Gospel:

> *And suddenly there was with the angel a multitude of the heavenly host praising God and **saying**: "Glory to God in the highest, and on earth peace, goodwill toward men!"* (Luke 2:13-14, emphasis mine)

The Bible says the angels *"said"* (but it does not say they *"sang"*): "Glory to God in the highest...." If the angels of Heaven were divided into thirds under the archangels according to their duties, then the third of the angels who followed satan in rebellion were probably *worship angels!* That left two-thirds of the angels remaining loyal to the Lord. So, remember, the angel who stands by *you* has already said no to the devil!

God Is Raising Up His Own Worship Team!

When God ejected satan and his cohorts, He was also dismissing the angelic worship team. As always, God already had a plan for a better replacement team that reflected His wisdom and glory in ways no created being could ever fathom. He would raise up a team of worshipers who would praise Him freely while wearing the linen white choir robes of the redeemed sprinkled with the crimson blood of their Redeemer!

Isn't it sad that in church we often quarrel over *the one thing that means the most to God?* Once again, we are talking about worship. He loves worship. It is the one thing that attracts Him to our gathering more than anything else. When God wanted to hear a song early in the first century, He had to invade a Philippian jail to hear two beaten preachers croak it out. He got so excited He patted His foot and triggered a massive earthquake![8]

If God wants to hear a song today, *He comes to church.* We can't afford to allow the corruption that removed worship from Heaven to get into our worship today! Satan knows this, so he will do anything he can to distract us from worship and incite us to criticize and divide. The Gospels tell the story of a man at Gadara with a legion of devils who immediately came to Jesus when His anointed foot touched the shore of that region. He had never seen or heard about Jesus, yet "something" drew him to the Master.

When he saw Jesus "from afar," he *ran* to meet the Lord so quickly that he met Jesus "immediately" after He landed! This man had approximately two thousand demons frantically clawing at his soul to keep him from responding to Jesus' presence. (There were at least enough demons to possess and destroy two thousand pigs. Who knows, some of those pigs may have had "double occupancy.")[9]

This demoniac was desperate for Jesus. He probably ran at least a mile to reach Jesus, and even though this man was full of frightened, desperate demons, he still managed to kneel down and worship Jesus! If two thousand demons couldn't keep a man from worshiping Jesus, how can we justify allowing so many unimportant things to keep *us* from worshiping Him?

Desire Will Find a Way, But Lack of Desire Will Find an Excuse

What does it take to draw us to the Lord? Are we so carried away by Him that just His presence leaves us breathless? Desire gave this unsaved, demonized man the power to overrule the will of the same two thousand demons that had ruled *his life* for years.

We need to know what kind of power we are dealing with in the demonic realm, and how it compares to the power of God in our lives. Godly knowledge about the adversary will remove all fear and transform the way we deal with demonic principalities and powers.

The Bible refers to satan in many ways, but in every case his status changed dramatically the day Jesus Christ rose from the dead in total victory. The Lord prophesied in advance through Ezekiel that one day He would personally destroy the devil.[10] The writer of Hebrews confirmed that through His own death, Jesus fulfilled divine prophecy and destroyed the devil, or "him who had the power of death..." (Heb. 2:14b).

Before His death on the cross, Jesus called satan "the prince of this world."[11] Paul described satan as "the god of this world" and "the ruler of darkness."[12] After Jesus died and rose again, the prince became the "has-been" prince of a defeated and condemned army. Things changed with the earthly arrival and victory of the King of kings and the Lord of lords. The victory is won, the decision is settled, and it is only a matter of time before the Victor returns for *all* of the spoils. Satan always wanted to be a king, but he only made it to the rank of prince over a kingdom he stole from Adam through deception. Now the only thing he will rule in eternity is a bottomless pit of damnation under the names of Abbadon and Apollyon.[13]

Have you heard people say, "I've been fighting the devil"? Don't believe it. It is the equivalent of a World War II soldier saying, "I've been fighting Hitler." Satan is not omnipresent, therefore, he accomplishes most of his mischief through underlings. That means when opposition comes against the gospel or the work of God, we are usually fighting lesser evil spirits. There is clearly a hierarchy of power in the ranks of hell. As you rise in the spirit, the size of your assignments in Christ increases—and so will the level or size of the demonic forces dispatched to hinder that work.

We Must Be Proficient at One Level Before Moving to the Next

God possesses all wisdom, and He requires us to become proficient at one level of obedience and faith before He moves us up to the next level. We can be confident in God's thoughts toward us. He said, "For I know the thoughts that I think toward you, says the Lord, thoughts of peace and not of evil, to give you a future and a hope" (Jer. 29:11). Best of all, Jesus promised He would never leave us or forsake us.[14]

Satan's real war is with God; we are not the primary target in his schemes. He assaults the people and purposes of God in the earth because he is powerless to hurt God. He has to settle for hurting God by hurting His people and by provoking them to disappoint God through disobedience or apathy. The devil is simply obsessed with the desire to insult the Bride of Christ.

Another aspect of satan is that he is a counterfeiter to the core. Paul spoke of "the mystery of Christ," referring to God's plan through Christ to reconcile to Himself *people of all races, tribes, and nations*, whether they were physically descended from Abraham or not.[15] Satan the counterfeiter responded with "the mystery of iniquity (or lawlessness)," which is simply the construction of a *false church* built with "power, signs, and lying wonders" alongside the true Church of God. This is the best the author of confusion could do.[16]

Satan's religious "church" of fallacy claims God's name but lives in sin, loves the world, and denies that God or His people have any real spiritual power.[17] The adversary may manage to fool a large percentage of people most of the time, but God knows those who are His own.

Don't sell the dominion Jesus restored to you on the cross. Everything that was lost due to Adam's sin in the beginning is available to us in Jesus Christ, the "second Adam" and the Lord of glory. The Bible says, "The kingdoms of this world have become the kingdoms of our Lord and of His Christ..." (Rev. 11:15b). The knowledge of the glory of God is going to cover the earth as the waters cover the sea.[18] What a day that will be!

Satan is presently the prince and power of the air; the Bible says he is lord/god of this world. He is also Beelzebub, lord of the flies. And think of the places where flies flock—places of rottenness and refuse. Finally, he's cast into a bottomless pit. His kingdom is in "free fall"—diminishing power, while Christ's Kingdom is ascending. Don't buy stock in the wrong kingdom!

The devil is still operating as the prince of the power of the air. In the eyes of the unredeemed world, he may still serve as their god of pleasure and self-gratification. However, his time is short and his power limited. God has given the Church authority over the "power behind the throne" in this world. This is yet another secret source of power to every child of the light and disciple of the King of kings and Lord of lords.

Endnotes

1. See Is. 14:12.
2. See Acts 16:16-18.

3. Adapted from the narratives found in Matthew 16:15-23, and Mark 8:29-33. It is interesting to note that the words Jesus used to rebuke satan in this incident involving Simon Peter are identical to the words He used to rebuke satan in the wilderness in Luke 4:8.

4. See Ezekiel 28:15.

5. See 2 Cor. 11:14.

6. See 2 Tim. 2:15.

7. Figures cited are based on a search of the *New King James Version of the Bible* using Parson's "QuickVerse 4.0" Bible software using the parameters specified

8. See Acts 16:23-26.

9. See Mk. 5:1-13.

10. See Ezek. 28:16.

11. See Jn. 14:30.

12. See 2 Cor. 4:4 KJV and Eph. 6:12, respectively.

13. See Rev. 9:11, 20:1-2.

14. See Heb. 13:5b.

15. See Eph. 3:3-4.

16. See 2 Thess. 2:7-9.

17. See 2 Tim. 3:1-9.

18. See Hab. 2:14.

Part IV

The Power of the Blood

*And thus you shall eat it: with a belt on your waist, your sandals on your feet, and your staff in your hand. So you shall eat it in haste. It is the Lord's Passover. For I will pass through the land of Egypt on that night, and will strike all the firstborn in the land of Egypt, both man and beast; and against all the gods of Egypt I will execute judgment: I am the Lord. Now the blood shall be a sign for you on the houses where you are. And **when I see the blood, I will pass over you;** and the plague shall not be on you to destroy you when I strike the land of Egypt* (Exodus 12:11-13).

Chapter 6

Purged and Preserved by Innocent Blood

No controversy in the history of man rages hotter than the heated controversy over the blood of Christ. The blood has always offended those with sins to hide and a rebellious will to protect, but few dreamed that it would become a point of offense among so many *in the churches* of America and Europe! The problem is that the blood not only saves the repentant, but it offends and condemns the defiant. It will never be popular among lovers of religion and the popularizers of "divinity through higher human expression and social evolution."

Many churches and respected theologians from the "best seminaries" decided the blood was "out" and the "greasy-grace, easy-sleazy social gospel" was "in" in the late 1800s. The message of "the blood" simply offended the sensibilities of too many civilized congregation members.

The accepted solution was to exchange the uncouth message of the blood for more palatable messages focusing on the more positive aspects of Jesus' teachings. The cross as a symbol of goodness was acceptable for display in church sanctuaries, lecterns, and church signs on the lawn—as long as no one brought up the bloody details of the Lord's passion on Calvary.

No! We should be frightened of a Christ-less, cross-less, bloodless Church. That would be the "perfect church" for satan, but it would do nothing for anyone descended from Adam. Whether it is considered politically correct, socially acceptable, or ministerial suicide, there must be an altar of death and a bloody sacrifice of flesh if we want salvation and power.

Most of us don't want to die, but death is required for those who would live. The bloodied Lamb left no room for debate or self-justification:

> *And he who does not take his cross and follow after Me is not worthy of Me. He who finds his life will lose it, and he who loses his life for My sake will find it* (Matthew 10:38-39).[1]

It seems we have become a little afraid of getting too bloody. Church leaders have said among themselves, "If we can handle this 'salvation thing' without blood, if we can make it as painless as possible, we would be so much more popular." Sorry, but there is no way to get around the blood.

To Live, You Must Find an Altar and Die

Truth, like freedom, is never won conclusively. It must be fought for by succeeding generations. There will be no victory without battle. The way of the cross is a bloody way. We should remember that it was a *gory* way before it became a *glory* way. No, dear friend, if you would live, then you must find an altar and die. A cross awaits you on the other side.

The offense of the blood can be traced to the time after the fall of Adam in the garden of Eden when God Himself shed the first blood to cover the sin of Adam and Eve. He killed an innocent animal to provide a covering or atonement for Adam and

Eve. The blood of the innocent for the guilty was required. From that day to this, man has had a built-in theology that without the shedding of blood there is no remission of sin (see Heb. 9:22).

God revealed a new and unspeakable secret about the blood when He engineered the exodus of the children of Israel from Egyptian bondage. He disclosed a new property of the blood of the innocent in the last plague He used to break the will of Pharaoh and punish Egypt for her mistreatment of Joseph's family. This secret is the basis for the Jewish observance of Passover and the foundation of our salvation in Christ.

The plagues that rocked Egypt had failed to shake Pharaoh's stubborn determination to hold the Hebrews in perpetual bondage. That brought Egypt to the final and worst plague of all. The time for the divine exodus was near, and justice would wait no longer. The Lord spoke to Moses and commanded every Israelite household in Goshen (the despised territory of shepherds inhabited by the Israelites), to slay a lamb without blemish and to apply its blood with a bunch of hyssop to the doorposts and lintels of their homes. Their orders were simple: *Stay in the house and stay under the blood.*[2]

God Said, "When I See the Blood..."

Then God explained that on that very night, the Death Angel would pass throughout the land of Egypt to strike down the firstborn of every household. The only thing that would save them from certain death was the power of the blood of a lamb. Then He said, *"When I see the blood, I will pass over you..."* (Ex. 12:13b).

This is the origin of the term, *passover*. Every house that was not covered by the blood suffered the death of its firstborn. There is no explanation for this. Human language falls short at this point. However, there is something about the blood of the lamb that attracts God. It excites Him and unleashes His highest thoughts, emotions, and power. If you want power with God, power for man, and power against satan, it all comes through the blood of the Lamb.

It is interesting to note that the Death Angel was an angel of God, but *even he could not cross the blood line!* If the angel of God cannot cross it, how much more will it be an impassable barrier to an agent of hell? It is the power in the blood.

There are three specific benefits provided by the blood of the lambs in Exodus 12:

1.   The blood protected them.

2.   The blood delivered them.

3.   The blood purged them from their past Egyptian history.

The Death Angel passed over the Israelites because of blood applied to their doorposts and lintels. Nothing moved Pharaoh to submit his will to God until blood was shed. The blood saved the repentant and damned the defiant. The blood "set at liberty the captives" in one night.

By the Blood, Through the Water, Under the Cloud, Full of the Lamb

God's instruction included the command that the Israelites eat their fill of the sacrificed lamb and unleavened bread in preparation for the exodus. That means the Israelites marched out of Egypt *by the blood,* through the water (of the Red Sea), under the cloud (of God's guiding presence), and full of the lamb that had been slain.

Make no mistake: The message of Exodus chapter 12 is as relevant to us today as it was to the Israelites long ago. If we are to be delivered out of the bondage of sin, we will get out by the shed blood of Jesus, through the water of baptism, under the cloud of God's glory, and full of the Lamb whose body was broken for us. There is power in the blood!

The sacrificed lamb even provided supernatural healing and health for the Israelites. Their deliverance prefigured much of what Christ did on the cross. The Psalmist declared there wasn't a sick person among the crowd of up to three-and-a-half million people![3]

Just think of a city of that size in America without a single case of back problems, headache, arthritis, cancer, or disability due to deformed limbs or malfunctioning muscles and nervous systems? Do you believe the Book? When the time for the exodus came, every descendant of Abraham walked out from under Egypt's shadow of bondage by the power of the blood of the lamb, and they walked out healed and delivered because they walked out through the door of blood.

Can you imagine what happened when the command came for the Israelites to be ready to leave? Don't you think someone said, "What are we going to do about Grandpa? He's so bent over he can't walk across the room, let alone out of Egypt!" About that time, they heard a loud "Snap! Crackle! Pop!" and then came Grandpa walking straight and ready to go! My friend, there is power in the blood.

The Infirm Danced Between the Bloodstained Posts

Can you imagine what happened to those who had suffered with twisted limbs all their lives? When the command came, "Go!" all of a sudden they felt waves of strength flow into their bodies and power came into their suddenly straightened and restored limbs. Suddenly they were healed! Those people didn't walk out of Egypt—they *danced* their way between the bloodstained posts into freedom. There is power in the blood.

The first Passover in Egypt began with a strange commission from the Lord, but something about the sacrifice of those innocent lambs was so precious to God that His Son took His name from what happened there. The instruction was to *slay a lamb* and apply its shed blood to the doorpost and lintel of every home. If you read the Scriptures, you will notice that if a family was too small or poor to afford a lamb, they could share a lamb and its blood with a neighbor.

Aren't you glad we can share the Lamb? The interesting thing was that the reverse was not true. Larger families were not required to kill more lambs—the blood of one lamb was sufficient, whether it was to cover a family of five or fifteen. The lamb was sufficient.

Even before the final plague came with the arrival of the Death Angel, each of the plagues sent against Egypt seemed to confirm the presence of an unseen, invisible division between Egypt and the children of Israel. Whether it was frogs or locusts, the Egyptians were overrun while the Israelites were untouched. At no time was this "dividing line" more apparent than the final night the Israelites spent under the bondage of Egypt, the night the Death Angel was unleashed against their captors. While the Israelites remained sheltered and safe under the protection of the blood, the wails and screams of heartbroken Egyptian households filled the land from border to border. This dividing line is virtually inexplicable except for the fact that there is power in the blood.

Their Captors Watched Them Splatter Blood on Their Doorposts

Until the plagues came, the Israelites were probably the laughingstock of the Egyptians. As the sun went down on that fateful last night, the Egyptians living nearest to the Israelites may have said among themselves, "What are those crazy Jews doing this time?" as they watched them splattering blood on their doorposts in the fading light. But centuries of spiritual, physical, and mental poverty ended that night. In a matter of hours, prison doors were opened and generations born in bondage were set free.

God used a unique word to describe the importance of the blood of those lambs in Egypt on the first Passover. He said, "The blood shall be a *sign* [or token] for you" (Ex. 12:13a). A "token" is a small part, a sign, or a symbol of something far greater. If just the merest token of the blood of a lamb accomplished what it did in Egypt before the birth, sacrificial death, and resurrection of Christ, what must the *real thing* be able to accomplish after Calvary? God wants us to find out.

Are we living beneath our privilege? Do we really understand how much the enemy fears the blood of Jesus? How often do we find ourselves at the enemy's mercy because we don't activate the power of the blood and use it by faith? How much do we suffer needlessly because we don't believe in it and exercise faith in its power? There is power in the blood—if we perceive it and apply it in our lives.

Even the lofty vision of Isaiah the prophet seemed to draw its power from an altar of bloody sacrifice. The prophet spoke of a burning coal from an altar that possessed the power to take away iniquity and purge away sin. Upon the death of King Uzziah, Isaiah had been looking at the king's empty throne when he seemed to lift his eyes above the throne to see another higher throne that was never empty. The prophet's vision was transported beyond the earthly into the heavenlies and he declared, "I saw the Lord sitting on a throne, high and lifted up, and the train of His robe filled the temple" (Is. 6:1b).

This too is a secret source of power. We must, first of all, personally see the Lord "high and lifted up" above all earthly potentates, heroes, champions, and thrones. As we pin our attention and affection on the exalted Lord, something from Heaven will begin to change our vision and transform our speech.

As You Exalt Him, Heaven Is Called to Attention

The prophet said that as he gazed at the One on the throne, the angels of Heaven were activated and a six-winged seraph flew to him. If you want to activate the high cherubs, the seraphim, and every other angel in Heaven's hierarchy, focus your gaze upon the lordship of Jesus. As you exalt Him, Heaven is called to attention. If you want Heaven and the angels and everything God has to move in your life, lift up your eyes and see the Lord, high and lifted up. Glorify Him and Heaven will visit you.

The seraph that flew to Isaiah carried with him a coal taken with tongs from the altar. When considering every scriptural reference and mention linking altars with the iniquities and sins of men, only one kind of altar seems to have the function of atonement, of taking away iniquity and purging sin. Could it be that this burning coal delivered by an angel came from a timeless brazen altar of sacrifice, an altar eternally splattered by the blood of the sacrificed Lamb of God who was slain before the foundations of the earth?

Victory Begins at a Bloody, Fiery Altar

If this was indeed a brazen altar (whether literal or figurative), then it was an altar where blood fell on coals of fire because it was a bloody altar of sacrifice. Victory begins at a bloody, fiery altar. Even though you see Him high and lifted up, you must also see the blood and fire of the altar of sacrifice.

You may or may not agree with this understanding of Isaiah's vision, but God doesn't waste words. In His divine plan, without the shedding of blood there is no remission (see Heb.

9:22). Isaiah cried out in open confession of sin, fearing for his life because his unredeemed flesh had seen the glory of the Lord. He needed his sins removed and his unworthiness *covered*. He needed the blood somehow, and perhaps the coal from the altar was a blood-stained coal of priceless worth.

THERE IS NO SHORTCUT AROUND CALVARY TO THE UPPER ROOM.

This explanation may not be to your satisfaction, but we must agree that it is dangerous for men to get to the fire before they get to the blood. According to the Book of Leviticus, Old Testament priests had to wring out the excess blood of certain animal sacrifices before they dragged the carcass across the altar. Again, we may be at the point of offense, but we have gone too far to turn back. Those priests, though dressed in white, had to bloody that altar from the bottom up and on all sides of the altar before they ever got to the fire. Offensive or not, this speaks loudly to any believer or church earnestly seeking revival today: *There is no shortcut around Calvary to the Upper Room.*

The apostle Paul speaks to each of us with this command: "I beseech you therefore, brethren, by the mercies of God, that you present your bodies a living sacrifice, holy, acceptable to God, which is your reasonable service" (Rom. 12:1). There must be a burning of self. The living offering must be placed on an altar of fire and fixed there with no escape. God's message has always been a message of blood first, and then of fire. That is the divine order of progression. You will never make it until you first bloody an altar somewhere. Lay your flesh out before God and make a personal trip to Calvary. Identify yourself with the Lamb of God who died there.

Consider the principle of miracle revealed in the way priests were to certify the cure of lepers among the Israelites. When a leper was finally cleansed, he was to go to the priest and bring with him two birds. The priest would pour water into a basin, kill one of the birds, and allow its blood to mix with the water. Then the priest would bind the living bird to a piece of wood and a sprig of hyssop using a piece of scarlet thread. Finally, the living bird was doused or "baptized" with the blood and water by the "tight hands of the law" represented by the priest.

Freed by the Death of Another

Immediately the quivering, frightened bird would be taken to an open field where it would be set free—all because of the wood, the hyssop, the scarlet thread, and the blood and water. The bird was *free because of the death of another kind like himself*. He was freed from the clutches of bondage and the law.

The water is part of the liberty. In the past, we were trapped and bound in the clutches of sin and ecclesiastical drudgery. We had no hope until the blood and the water and a Substitute took away our sentence of death. It was no accident that when a soldier pierced Jesus' side on the cross, a mixture of blood and water came forth.

Though we were quivering and fearful in the hands of the Law, each of us can confidently say, "With an old piece of wood from Calvary, with the scarlet thread of my sin and guilt, with the hyssop of my cleansing, and still dripping from my baptism in the blood and water from Christ's side, they took me out into an open field and set me free!" For good reason the Lamb of God declared, "Therefore if the Son makes you free, you shall be free indeed" (Jn. 8:36).

Those who would light their fires in the house of God should remember every flame of the tabernacle of old *had to be ignited from the fire of the brazen or bloody altar*. Otherwise it was "strange fire," and strange fire is more dangerous to man than no fire at all. Make sure you do not light your fires on anything less than the bloody altar of Calvary. Settle for nothing less than the power of the blood in your life!

The blood of Christ is vital to the life and vitality of the Church. We simply can't afford to be squeamish or "civilized" when it comes to the blood. The writer of Hebrews asked, "How much more shall the blood of Christ, who through the eternal Spirit offered Himself without spot to God, *cleanse your conscience from dead works* to serve the living God?" (Heb. 9:14)

Take the Bloody Beaten Path to the Mercy Seat

Only the blood of Christ can purge us from "dead works of the flesh." Could that sense of dullness in our Christian lives and service come from our lack of knowledge about the bloody beaten path to the mercy seat? Trust God's Word. You will come alive to Him if you will allow the blood of Christ to cut away that old deadness and dullness. When you are inundated with the blood of the Lamb, you will finally be like the little bird who escaped bondage and death to break loose and experience true freedom.

It is time for us to find a place at the bloody altar and identify ourselves with the Lamb of God. It is here that we will renew our experience with Him in prayer. Prayers are answered through the blood. It can still destroy plagues, stop demons, and mark a divine dividing line between the holy and the profane, the repentant and the proud.

We must put away the plagues created by our murmuring and lethargy, by our unwilling ways and lack of concern. It is time to die to self and live in Him; it is time to be baptized in the cleansing blood of Christ and the water of the Holy Spirit at an old-fashioned altar of prayer. We must journey to the cross and say before the Lord, "I accept all that is of God. I refuse all that is not of God. I put it all under the blood of the Lord Jesus Christ."

The writer of Hebrews declared:

Therefore, brethren, having boldness to enter the Holiest **by the blood of Jesus, by a new and living way** *which He consecrated for us, through the veil, that is, His flesh, and having a High Priest over the house of God, let us draw near with a true heart in full assurance of faith, having our hearts sprinkled from an evil conscience and our bodies washed with pure water* (Hebrews 10:19-22).

The way of the blood, the path of the cross, is not a dead way. Unlike the churches man has built using the pattern of the Law and human whims, the true Church is not a way of drudgery and tradition. The Lamb has been slain, the blood was shed, and the "veil" of His flesh was rent.

We are told that when Jesus died, the veil in the temple was rent or torn to *let everyone into the Holiest of Holies.* A careful study of the furniture of the tabernacle reveals that it has always been described from the Holiest of Holies *outward.* Could this be symbolic of God's desire to reach out for humanity, not of humanity reaching for God?

Perhaps Jesus' bloody sacrifice on Calvary was less a way of opening the Holy of Holies to everyone and more a way of God saying, "Let Me out of this little religious box. Let Me get out to where the people are. I am no longer satisfied with the worship and intimate companionship of only one man one time a year. I am after a people, a kingdom of kings and priests...." Maybe this is why the Book of Revelation says of Jesus Christ the Lamb:

You were slain, and have redeemed us to God by Your blood out of every tribe and tongue and people and nation, and have made us kings and priests to our God; and we shall reign on the earth (Revelation 5:9b-10).

Jesus' wounded side is open. Blood and water pour forth and you have an invitation to walk through the wound to the very heart of God.

Kindred Blood Graced His Entrance...

About 20 years ago, a very important meeting convened in the executive boardroom of a large church organization. The issues of the day were vital and the discussions were strictly confidential. The chairman of the board was explaining some key points when in the midst of the proceedings the door to the boardroom was suddenly flung open.

How could it have happened? Whoever it was had to have passed through the gauntlet of a seasoned secretary, a protective administrative aide, and negotiated two doors and a flight of stairs to get to the meeting room. The secretary had not called, nor had the administrative aide stepped in to get authorization for the intrusion.

When the door opened, every eye turned to watch a four-year-old child confidently cross the room, totally oblivious to every face but one. When the little arms went up, the chairman quickly took his grandson into his arms and gave him the hug he was looking for. When that little boy had learned that his "Pawpaw" was upstairs in a meeting, he pressed his way past every obstacle. Do you know what happened? The meeting halted and Pawpaw gave him all his attention. *Kindred blood graced his entrance.* Everything else took second place in order of importance as the author's grandson, Shane, received his hug.

It doesn't matter what God is doing—He could be ruling the universe, hanging out stars, or painting galaxies; but when one of His own blood-washed children opens the door to the throne room to talk to Daddy, the angels step aside. He recognizes us as His children and He has given us a blood right to walk through the wound of the Lamb into the very heart of God. What greater source of power could we ask for?

Endnotes

1. Also see Mt. 16:25, Mk. 8:35, and Lk. 9:24; 17:33.
2. See Ex. 12:1-22.
3. See Ps. 105:37.

Chapter 7

Armed With the Blood of the Lamb

There is power in the blood of the Lamb, but that power is useless if we neglect to use it. Our concept of the blood cannot become strictly a theological position. Satan isn't afraid of theology, and he has even less fear of theologians—unless they are washed in the blood and know how to use the blood of Christ as a weapon.

Life is in the blood. Everything we believe and teach and hope for is tied to the power of the blood of the Lamb, Christ Jesus. Yet it is not enough for us to say we believe in the literal, actual shedding of the blood of Jesus and that without that shedding of blood we have no hope. All we have done is take a theological position that is firmly based on Scripture. That is good and necessary, but is simply not enough!

We must know and experience this truth in the twenty-first century! Somehow this truth must become a "heart passion" that affects every part of our lives. The blood of Christ is *more* than a vital part of our salvation. It is a weapon meant to be used for both defense and offense. We need to learn how to activate, move, and flow in the power of the blood in our daily lives.

The Israelites in Egypt lived through a beautiful object lesson in the power of the blood and of God's protection. In plague after plague, no matter how much chaos swept through Egypt or what traumatized the Egyptians around them, nothing could cross the dividing line protecting God's people.

Presently we live in chaotic days marked by wars and rumors of wars, earthquakes, economic crises, and plagues of all kinds. Yet we too have a crimson dividing line separating the redeemed from the lost. We are "living through" an object lesson of our own if we have eyes to see and ears to hear: How beautiful it is to know that our lives are hid with God beneath the blood of the Lamb.

The Power of the Blood Goes *Beyond* Sin

The writer of Hebrews declared, "...according to the law almost all things are purified with blood, and without shedding of blood there is no remission" (Heb. 9:22). Notice the passage does not say "remission of *sin*." Sin is definitely included, but the power of the blood does not end when it takes care of sin. It purges *almost* everything. Without the shedding of blood there is no remission.

Priests in the Old Testament sprinkled almost everything with blood. What wasn't sprinkled with blood was dabbed with anointing oil. They had complete confidence in the power of the blood to cleanse, deliver, protect. *It was a total purgative.* It was the key to remission and pardon and liberty.

Luke often used the word *remission* in his Gospel or record of the Good News. According to his report, Jesus Himself implied that it was to be part of what we call "the apostle's doctrine" when He said, "...repentance and remission of sins should be preached in His name to all nations... (Lk. 24:47).

Luke was a physician, and the medical concept of "remission" meant then what it means now. If someone with a malignancy or disease in their body experiences a significant improvement in their condition, they are said to be "in remission." It means the disease process has been arrested or is in retreat.

The Blood Forces the Works of the Flesh Into Remission

The blood of the Lamb attacks sin and chases it away. Sin retreats in the presence of the washing of the blood of Jesus. The works of the flesh go in remission when the power of the blood drives them out. There is good reason for the enemy to fear the blood. Even sin recognizes the blood. The demons of hell quake and tremble at the mention of the blood of the Lamb.

We must learn the principles that lead to the release of the power of the blood in our lives. We face days of unparalleled destiny for the Church in the midst of unparalleled darkness. We need to recognize the efficacy, or the force and power of the blood in our day and time.

> THE BLOOD OF THE LAMB DOES MORE THAN SIMPLY DELIVER US FROM SIN; ITS POWER COVERS AND PROTECTS.

The Lord said to the Israelites, "For *the life of the flesh is in the blood, and I have given it to you upon the altar to make atonement for your souls; for it is the blood that makes atonement for the soul*" (Lev. 17:11). The word *atonement* means "covering."

The blood of the Lamb does more than simply deliver us from sin; its power covers and protects. Even more than that, it is a tool and a weapon we can use to deliver, cover, and protect others.

When God told Moses about the "dividing line" or "division" He would put around the Israelites in Egypt, He used a very specific word that is important to our understanding of the power of the blood. He said, "And I will put a *division* between My people and thy people" (Ex. 8:23a KJV). (The New King James Version says, "I will make a *difference*....") The Hebrew of that passage reads, "I will put *redemption* between My people and thy people." The power of the blood preempts and protects us from the plagues of the devil.

I Plead the Blood!

Some of the old-timers from the early days of the Pentecostal outpouring used to frequently say, "I plead the blood! I plead the blood of Jesus!" This powerful phrase needs to be restored to our vocabulary because there is still power in that blood.

Several years ago a man and his wife were in a very serious car accident.[1] When the man came to himself, he realized his wife was bleeding profusely next to him. As people started to rush to the car to see if they could help, he reached over and laid his hand on his wife who was literally bleeding to death. People who were strangers to God's way walked up and heard him saying, "I plead the blood. I plead the blood. I plead the blood."

He testifies today that Jesus' blood flow stopped his wife's blood flow! The people who gathered around the couple that day didn't understand what was happening, but the angels of God and the Almighty Himself certainly understood his language. Their lives were spared because there is healing and delivering power in the blood!

The same man served as Foreign Missions Director of his denomination in the late '60s and '70s. Frequently his travels took him to Asia and Africa, and he noticed that on occasion, the strange demons from a foreign country would follow him home! He said, "I had fought them all night long, and there were some strange ones. In the middle of the night they would wake me up. I would hear my children wake up crying because of a spiritual attack of fear, and not knowing why they were afraid. They didn't know, but I did. Not that I was a spiritual giant, I just would know exactly what it was."

He said he would get up and go through his house from room to room, being careful not to skip "one nook or cranny"—and plead the blood of Jesus: "I plead the blood! I plead the blood!" He commanded in the name of Jesus and by the power of the blood that every evil spirit return from whence it came. The peace of God would always flood the house as the enemy forces had to make their exit. The man was T.F. Tenney.

The blood protects—the blood purges—the blood is victorious. The events of the first Passover proved that even the Death Angel has to back up when he sees the power of the blood of the Lamb.

The Blood Speaks Better Things...

Did you know the blood talks? According to the writer of Hebrews, "The blood of sprinkling [the blood of Jesus]...speaks better things than that of Abel" (Heb. 12:24b). According to the Bible, the "blood" we are talking about is *the blood of God*.[2] In other words, *the only blood God ever had flowed through the veins of Jesus Christ*. The power of the blood sealed Christ's victory at Calvary.

An agnostic would have us believe that if Jesus is truly God and if Jesus died, then God died at Calvary. The objection is simple: *All of God that could die, died at Calvary*. We are speaking of the flesh of the Lamb slain before the foundation of the earth.

We must have vital faith in the precious blood of Jesus. It is not enough to simply repeat the rhetoric or say the words, "I plead the blood." It is believing something happens when you say it. "I plead the blood of Jesus! It talks for me! It will slap the devil right in the face for me."

When the enemy extends his clammy hand toward some area of your life, a voice you didn't hear booms into satan's darkness just as he is ready to close his grip. "Get your hands off My child!" Immediately the devil's grip loosens. He says to himself, "Oh no! I recognize that voice. It is the voice of the blood of the Lamb. I cannot do this. I can stay out here and howl and froth and lie and try to frighten this man, but I cannot lay my hand on him. It's not fair. He is under the blood and I cannot go there."

For 15 centuries, Israel had a sanctuary containing a special area called the Holy of Holies. It would mean death to anyone, except the priest, who entered that place. It had one message and it was simple: Man cannot dwell in the presence of Almighty God.

Christ Shed His Blood for All— Even Those Who Reject Him

God Himself changed that by firmly planting the cross of Calvary into the bedrock of the human experience, anchored to the needs of earth. The cross pointed upward while reaching perpendicular to the heavens. This symbolized the power of Christ's work on the cross to bring the needs of earth to Heaven. Jesus hung on that tree with one bloody arm extended out to a thief who accepted His invitation to forgiveness and eternal life. Without favoritism, the other bloody arm also extended to one whom He knew was going to reject His offer. It didn't matter to the Redeemer; He shed His blood for all. He reaches for both categories of people—the acceptors and the rejectors—with His scarred and loving arms. He made a new and living way where there was no way.

Take the limits off the atonement. Embrace the power of the blood of the Son of God. He said, "And I, if I be lifted up from the earth, will draw all men unto me" (Jn. 12:32 KJV). There is nothing God cannot do through the power of the blood of His Majesty, the Lord Jesus Christ.

The Book of Revelation mentions "...the great city which spiritually is called Sodom and Egypt, where also our Lord was crucified" (Rev. 11:8). No, this is not some translation error. We know Jesus was not crucified in Egypt or in Sodom. God mentioned these cities as a way to say this: When Jesus died on Calvary, the power of the blood washed all the way to the first Passover lamb that was slain in Egypt. It planted a cross there that proclaims its sovereignty over everything that ancient Egypt represents. The blood then looked at the depths of sin but couldn't find a place lower than Sodom to which to flow. He then said, "I will plant a cross even in that cursed cesspool of iniquity and debauchery. Yes, 'The blood can take care of even this.'"

Take the limits off the atonement. Paul named virtually everything in the catalog of sin in his letter to the Corinthians when he wrote:

*Neither fornicators, nor idolaters, nor adulterers, nor homosexuals, nor sodomites, nor thieves, nor covetous, nor drunkards, nor revilers, nor extortioners will inherit the kingdom of God. **And such were some of you. But you were washed,** but you were sanctified, but you were justified in the name of the Lord Jesus and by the Spirit of our God* (1 Corinthians 6:9b-11).

When the apostle said, "Such were some of you," the message was simple: You were all those things, but you have been washed in the blood of a spotless Lamb. You have been set apart, reserved, and made right with God in the name of Jesus and by the spirit of our God. Thank God for the blood!

There Is Power in the Blood

Review this brief survey of the blood in the Bible and remember there is power in the blood:

1. It is the *blood* that makes atonement (see Lev. 17:11).

2. It is the *blood* that causes judgment, death, and calamity to pass over you. (The promise of Exodus 12:13 is: "When I see the *blood*, I will pass over you.")

3. The *blood* ended your exile and constantly draws you close to God (see Eph. 2:17).

4. The *blood* gives you boldness to enter the Holy of Holies (see Heb. 10:19).

5. It was the precious *blood* of Jesus that redeemed you (see 1 Pet. 1:18-19).

6. The *blood* of Jesus Christ cleanses you from all sin (see 1 Jn. 1:7).

7. It is by the *blood of the Lamb* that you overcome (see Rev. 12:11)!

Thank God for the blood! It protects. It delivers. It purges. If you are depressed, plead the blood. If you are sick, plead the blood. If you are fearful, plead the blood. In Jesus' name, may you be bound to the liberating power of the blood of the Lamb!

Endnotes

1. This man is Rev. T.F. Tenney, coauthor of *Secret Sources of Power* and father of Tommy Tenney.
2. See Acts 20:28.

Part V

The Power of Relinquishment

Now it came to pass in those days, when Moses was grown, that he went out to his brethren and looked at their burdens. And he saw an Egyptian beating a Hebrew, one of his brethren. So he looked this way and that way, and when he saw no one, he killed the Egyptian and hid him in the sand. And when he went out the second day, behold, two Hebrew men were fighting, and he said to the one who did the wrong, "Why are you striking your companion?" Then he said, "Who made you a prince and a judge over us? Do you intend to kill me as you killed the Egyptian?" So Moses feared and said, "Surely this thing is known!" (Exodus 2:11-14)

*Then Moses answered and said, "But suppose they will not believe me or listen to my voice; suppose they say, 'The Lord has not appeared to you.'" So the Lord said to him, "What is that in your hand?" He said, "A rod." And He said, "**Cast it on the ground.**" So he cast it on the ground, and it became a serpent; and Moses fled from it. Then the Lord said to Moses, "Reach out your hand and take it by the tail" (and he reached out his hand and* *caught it, and it became a rod in his hand), "that they may believe that the Lord God of their fathers, the God of Abraham, the God of Isaac, and the God of Jacob, has appeared to you." Furthermore the Lord said to him, "Now put your hand in your bosom." And he put his hand in his bosom, and when he took it out, behold, his hand was leprous, like snow. And He said, "Put your hand in your bosom again." So he put his hand in his bosom again, and drew it out of his bosom, and behold, it was restored like his other flesh (Exodus 4:1-7).*

Chapter 8

Relinquished to the Process of God

When God decided to reveal another facet of His divinity to Abraham and his son Isaac, He did it while taking them through a divine process of preparation we will call "relinquishment." This is the process of releasing, yielding, resigning, surrendering, abandoning, waiving, and giving up something completely.

There is power in relinquishment, but the process isn't much fun at times. It took Isaac up the slopes of Mt. Moriah and left him tied to an altar like a lamb led to slaughter. He wondered if he would live to see the sunset, and he probably wondered why it happened to him. The whole situation was a result of something he had nothing to do with! Isaac didn't know in advance what role he would play in God's purposes, so *all he could do was relinquish himself to the process.*

Abraham didn't understand what was going on either. God's request that he sacrifice Isaac was totally out of character with the God he had known in the past. All Abraham could do was relinquish his son and trust God. By faith, he must have said, "Lord, if I kill Isaac, I know You are able to raise him from the dead. Your word is true and You promised me You would make a mighty nation out of him." Can you imagine the load Abraham carried up that mountain?

Moses could speak to us about relinquishment too. He knew God had called him to deliver the children of Israel, but he wanted to do it his own way. He was wearing the clothing of a prince of Egypt when he went sauntering forth and saw an opportunity. He saw an Egyptian beating a Hebrew slave and this deliverer decided it was time to rise to the occasion and take things into his own hands. At the end of the story a man was dead. That is the Egyptian way.

God Will Let You Do Things Your Way (and Let You Pay for It)

Moses was about to learn that God will not use an unwilling servant. If you want something badly enough that God has withheld from you, then God will let you have it. He will not fight you for the relinquishment of your will. If you want to take things in your own hands and do things your own way, God will allow you to do so. He will step back and say, "Okay, go ahead." The Israelites found out the hard way:

> *They soon forgot His works; They did not wait for His counsel, but lusted exceedingly in the wilderness, and tested God in the desert. And **He gave them their request, but sent leanness into their soul*** (Psalm 106:13-15).

Moses' "Egyptian way" is never what God has in mind. The Bible tells us that Moses "looked this way and that way" before he murdered the Egyptian.[1] *What he failed to do was look up!* He wanted to know if men were looking and evidently he wasn't concerned by the fact that God was watching. God said, "Okay, Moses. The first thing I have to teach you is where you get your orders. You won't be so interested in audience response then. It matters little if anyone is watching."

Moses probably thought he had done a good deed. After all, he had saved an Israelite. Perhaps he even told himself, "One down; ten million to go." Then Moses dug a little hole and *buried his mistake in the sand.*

Not too many days passed before God openly exposed the works of Moses' flesh and made it known. Once he stepped out of the will of God, Moses couldn't even keep one Egyptian buried in the sand. *When he stepped back into the will of God, however, he was able to bury the entire army of Pharaoh in the bed of the Red Sea!* Moses tackled a job doing it one at a time, but he didn't do it in God's time or God's way. God had a better plan, a better time, and a better way.

Do You Have Your B.N. Degree?

Moses, the prince in Egypt, thought he was going to become a missionary, but instead he became a murderer. He promptly became a fugitive without a home. The man with a Ph.D. in Egyptology had the wrong bones excavated (the man he killed) and found himself on the backside of a desert working on his B.N. degree (a "Be Nothing" degree). He was in the depths of the process of relinquishment!

At this stage in his life, Moses was a man who was "stuffed full of himself." It is hard for God to fill a man who is full to overflowing with himself. We will never mature or come into power with God until we come to the end of ourselves and are willing to relinquish everything to Him.

It has been observed that there were three basic phases in Moses' life:

1. Moses spent the first 40 years of his life learning to be a prince in the house of Pharaoh.

2. He spent the second 40 years learning to be a pauper.

3.   The final 40 years of his life, Moses learned to be a prophet.

Some people would say the first 40 years Moses learned something and the next 40 years he learned nothing. Actually, Moses learned the value of humility in the wilderness school of relinquishment. That is what qualified him for the third set of 40 years, when Moses learned what God could do with a man who had learned the first two lessons!

The time will come when each of us will fully realize that we are at the end of ourselves. It is then that the power of relinquishment can come into play in our lives. A popular phrase is used a lot, particularly by the young and by the discontented: "I'm going to make something of myself." People usually say that while thinking of specific talents, abilities, or specific educational goals. They may be noble goals, but it may shock you to know that basically, that is not what God wants.

WANTED: Baptized Brains

God is not against education—He can use baptized brains. Perhaps we should tell young people: "Get a good education and get over it." The truth is that God cannot use your education until something "happens" to you. Until self is under control and Jesus is on the throne of our lives, we are powerless where Heaven is concerned. Power in God's Kingdom only comes with relinquishment.

When you come to the end of yourself—the end of your road—you've driven up into God's front yard! It happened to Moses. After he did things "his way," he found himself running for his life as an exiled prince of Egypt. Moses ended up living on the backside of the desert tending sheep, even though he had been trained like any good Egyptian to hate sheep and hate shepherds with equal enthusiasm. That means Moses' sins took him from the house of the Pharaoh to the very lowest of the low.

In other words, God was rubbing Moses' face in the mess he had made.

He jerked Moses away from Pharaoh's throne and removed him from the affluence and influence of Pharaoh's court. Then He brought him to the desert and required him to do the very thing he had been taught to hate. When God gets ready to develop something in you, don't be surprised when He introduces you to His unique "relinquishment process" for success.

For 40 years, this process required Moses to follow bleating sheep and learn every back road, spring, and oasis in the Sinai Desert. He didn't realize it, but he was being given knowledge and experience he would need in his future to fulfill God's plan. The apostle Paul referred to this process when he said, "We may be able to comfort those who are in any trouble, with the comfort with which we ourselves are comforted by God" (2 Cor. 1:4b).

Be Prepared to Give Someone Your Yesterday Today

Sometimes we go through things not so much for us but for the sake of someone else. *Your yesterday may be someone else's today.* God may be preparing you to feed their today out of your experiences of yesterday. That doesn't mean you won't wonder why such things are happening to you at the time.

Hindsight is an invaluable way to learn how things fit into God's plan. There is no such thing as "waste" in God's economy. He knows exactly what He is doing. God led Moses the prince of Egypt and murderer into the desert to teach him how to be a shepherd and deliverer. It was in the "desert of relinquishment" that Moses learned many of the things he needed to lead Israel through the Sinai. Moses wasn't thrilled about going back to Egypt and all of its memories. He wanted to have a pity party but no one showed up but the devil. (That is what usually happens at pity parties.)

David was also familiar with the process of relinquishment. He was the one who wrote, "Yea, though I walk through the valley of the shadow of death…" (Ps. 23:4). Each one of us will experience our own valleys and feel the cold shadow of death on our shoulders at times. David, the same man who lived in a cave as an exile and outlaw, and later ran for his life when his own son plotted to kill him, has some words of wisdom for us.

The Psalmist who endured decades of "relinquishment" while running from Saul's armies said, "If you are in the valley of the shadow, just keep walking. What you need is an uninterrupted walk with God, even if He takes you through the dark valley. Just don't wallow in it. Don't linger there. Don't pitch your tent under that shadow. Above all, don't throw a pity party in that valley."

Say "Here I Am" to Find Out Who You Are

Moses discovered that the process of relinquishment could transform his strengths into weaknesses and his weaknesses into strengths. When Moses turned aside to investigate the burning bush on Mount Sinai, God called out to him from the bush and Moses said, "Here am I" (Ex. 3:4b KJV). Only seven verses later, Moses was saying, "Who am I…?" (Ex. 4:11b)

You will never find out who you are until you say to God, "Here I am." We must offer ourselves first. It is no good trying to find out what God wants *first,* and then deciding whether or not we are willing. We must offer ourselves unconditionally and simply say, "Here I am." This is what it means to relinquish ourselves to Him, and this is what releases the *power* of God in our lives.

God was patient with His reluctant deliverer. Moses didn't start by parting the Red Sea. He had to begin by taking small, tentative steps of faith to relinquish his fears and take hold of God's ability. "Moses, what is in your hand?" God asked. We know it was just a rod, a shepherd's staff, a mere stick. Yet that stick became a miracle *when Moses turned it loose* at God's command. When did it cease to be a miracle? The miraculous stopped and the mundane began when Moses picked it back up. *That is the power of relinquishment.*

It was customary for a shepherd in the time of Moses and David to whittle and carve his stories or personal history into the beam of his staff. Then it was passed from generation to generation as a family heirloom. When God said to Moses, "Give me your staff," it was as if He was saying, *"Give me your past."* It was the last symbol of authority.

Moses left his scepter in Egypt. By then, the staff was the symbol of his authority over those bleating sheep. God was now saying, "Give Me your authority! Throw that down, too." Moses could have said, "You've already taken everything from me. I need this staff to lean on," but he chose to relinquish his past and embrace the will of God.

The Lord says to each of us, "Turn it loose if you want to be what I want you to be." It is in those moments that we discover the power of relinquishment. Only when everything and everyone but God is gone do we realize that God is enough.

Up Is Down and You Die to Live

Jesus said, "If anyone desires to be first, he shall be last of all and servant of all" (Mk. 9:35b). In God's economy, up is down and the way you live is to die. The way you get is to give because the laws of the Kingdom are reversed from the laws of this world. According to the law, in the shadow of Egypt you must grab and climb, regardless of who you step on. That just won't work if you import it into the church setting—you have to turn it loose.

God expects us to do some things for ourselves, but sometimes we get out of control and try to do everything ourselves. We must replace our stubborn compulsion to do our own thing with a willingness to "let go." Sin began because the devil said, "I will." Redemption was birthed because Jesus said, "Not My will, but Yours, be done" (Lk. 22:42b).

Paul knew how to relinquish things to God. He said, "And I will very gladly spend and be spent for your souls; though the more abundantly I love you, the less I am loved" (2 Cor. 12:15). Paul wasn't offering a little here and a little there, a little now and a little later. He was offering everything unreservedly.

We don't mind the part about "spending and being willing to spend." We just have problems when we become the "currency" and the "being spent" part starts. Relinquishment comes into play when God starts taking things out of you and taking them away from you. Paul, for instance, had to learn how to love without being loved back. None of us like that part.

Moses was scrambling for excuses to avoid God's call when the Lord told him, "Okay, now put your hand in your bosom...now pull it out." Moses was shocked to see that his hand was covered with leprosy! What did he do to deserve that? Perhaps God wanted Moses to know that He knew there had been a little sin on those hands. "Put it back, now out again." When Moses withdrew his hand again, his skin was perfectly clean and clear again.

God was teaching Moses two lessons. First, any person who cannot control the flesh, cannot cast out the devil. You must know what is in your heart and keep your flesh clean through repentance and obedience. Then you can handle the devil.

The Controlling Hand Is a Powerless Hand

Moses, put your hand on your heart. It will reveal what is hidden in your hands. The second lesson was that God cannot do miracles through anyone who wants control. God let Moses know who was in charge and where the power came from.

God intended to embarrass the devil and humble Pharaoh, but first He had to work on Moses' attitude. You will never be a success for the Kingdom until you see yourself as a threat to the enemy. We are more of a threat to him than he can be to us—when we relinquish ourselves to God.

You can be sure the process of relinquishment and preparation in life can get confusing at times. Moses tried to lead the children of Israel out of Egypt but things suddenly took a turn toward disaster. He and the Israelites ended up at the shore of the Red Sea with Pharaoh's army hot on their heels. Pharaoh had just come from the deathbed of his firstborn and there was vengeance in his eyes and violence in his heart. His pursuit of the Jewish people was relentless, and Moses knew he was coming.

The people said, "We ought to go *back* to Egypt."

Moses said, "*Stand still.*"

God said, "*Go forward.*"

Sometimes we find ourselves in a similar place. People around us ask, "What are you doing moving in *that* direction? Go back to where you were comfortable." Meanwhile, a leader you respect may say, "Maybe you ought to just stay put for awhile. Maybe the timing is just not right." The only way to find your way among conflicting opinions is to ask this question: What does *God* say? "Go forward."

Don't Date Power While Leaving Purity at Home

We have a habit of wanting power without inviting its twin sister, purity. You cannot buy power at the cost of purity. Power is only safe in the balancing presence of uncompromising purity. Judge nothing before its time, and don't rush into things before you've "gone through the fires of purity." You do not have to lose your purity to increase your power.

As we move forward through the wilderness of relinquishment, we must remember that faith is the currency of God's Kingdom. He isn't "indebted" to us; He is indebted to our *faith*. With faith we can buy anything God has. He is not impressed by the longevity of our prayers, even though prayer is a prerequisite to a successful Christian walk. What moves God is faith. Consecration does not move Him, even though consecration is an honorable thing. We must believe that He can before He will.

Keepers Weepers, Losers Finders

Children at play like to say, "Finders keepers, losers weepers!" Jesus said, "Whoever loses his life will find it." The law of His Kingdom is "keepers weepers, losers finders." The power of relinquishment is released when you pray, "Father, I give You my self, my reputation, my education, my past, my future, and my present. I want the very best You have for me."

You must keep praying until you reduce all your desires into one—to serve the Lord with all your heart, soul, and might. Pray until all your fear is reduced to one fear—the fear of the Lord. In that moment you will experience a glorious liberty. As for the "rod in your hand," the ordinary tools of service God put in your life, they will be transformed into the "rod of God."

Moses' rod was once a simple shepherd's crook, a tool for herding sheep and steadying the shepherd's step in places of uncertain footing. When Moses learned to fear God more than man and laid down his rod at God's command, the Lord took ownership of Moses' rod and used it to miraculously deliver the children of Israel from their bondage. God seeks ordinary people who will simply relinquish themselves to Him. It is truly amazing what God will do when we make ourselves genuinely available to Him.

Two of the ordinary people used by God in the Old Testament participated in one of the strangest battles ever fought in the history of man. When the men of Amalek decided to pick a fight with Moses and the Israelites, Moses told a man named Joshua to pick out some men and "go fight with Amalek tomorrow." The only reassurance he gave Joshua was this: "Tomorrow I will stand on the top of the hill with the rod of God in my hand" (Ex. 17:9b). Joshua's chief credential was that he served Moses faithfully as his assistant.

Meanwhile, a second ordinary man named Hur climbed a hill with Moses and Aaron the high priest. As long as Moses held up the rod of God in his hand, then Joshua and the Israelites won. When the rod went down the Amalekites prevailed.

Joshua could have looked up from the battlefield and said, "Moses, why don't *you* come down here and fight?" but he didn't. Had he done it, Moses would have said, "I *am* fighting here. It is just a different kind of fight."

Faithfully Lift Up the Rod God Gave You

The same thing could be said for saints who patiently and faithfully intercede for various enterprises and people in the Kingdom of God. Each time they pray, they lift up the rod God gave them, the rod of prayer. They know Paul was right—"For the weapons of our warfare are not carnal..." (2 Cor. 10:4). No matter what rod God puts in your hand, you can be assured that it is a rod of victory and a rod of battle.

If you cannot be the leader, then you need to help the leader succeed. Jesus said the greatest leaders in the Kingdom are those who serve. The success of one is the success of all in the Body of Christ. When Moses could no longer hold up the rod of God, he sat down on a rock and Aaron and Hur stepped in to hold up his arms and the rod of God.

Did you know that this is the only record of anything Hur ever accomplished? And we discover this much: His children and grandchildren were greatly used in the Tabernacle, and were known for their faithfulness.[2] We remember Hur as only "the man who held up his pastor's arms." Yet, because he did that simple task, he imparted a spirit into his children and grandchildren that elevated them to positions of great authority and responsibility. Hur was faithful to hold up the hands of the man of God who was his leader. That spirit of loyalty and support was transmitted through his children for at least two generations.

There is a lesson to be learned here: The process of relinquishment always seems to require us to hold up the hands of our pastor or leader. Whether you are called to preach the gospel, teach a Sunday school class, or be an effective witness in your business office or in your neighborhood, don't be surprised if God asks you to lay down your rod or gift long enough to help your pastor by doing something for him that he just doesn't have time to do. Don't keep thinking, *That's not my* job.... Just as the disciples in Acts appointed others to wait tables in order to give themselves to prayer and the Word, so you should do all you can to free your pastor to do the same.

Endnotes

1. See Ex. 2:12.
2. See Ex. 31:2-11, 35:30-35; 1 Kings 4:7-8.

Chapter 9

Empty Yourself, Be Filled With God's Power

It is said the average American speaks nine million words a year. Five million of those words are the words, *I, me, my,* or *mine.* It is a staggering statistic. It tells you something about the spirit of the age in which we live. It is a selfish age. All truth is parallel. God's solution for selfishness is death to self. Why should we be surprised when God calls for selfless leaders in a selfish age?

And whoever desires to be first among you, let him be your slave; just as the Son of Man did not come to be served, but to serve, and to give His life a ransom for many (Matthew 20:27-28).

Disciples are expected to live with a deeper level of relinquishment than new believers. In the same way, those who would lead and feed must relinquish more than they did as disciples.

Moses was fed at Pharaoh's table and he was subjected to the disciplines of the Egyptian royal house. He was educated and trained in all the ways of Egypt. This discipline took Moses to a high level of accomplishment in Egyptian society, but it counted for almost nothing in God's Kingdom. According to the Book of Acts, Moses was "learned in all the wisdom of the Egyptians, and was mighty in words and deeds" *until his 40th birthday* when he decided to visit his Hebrew brethren (see Acts 7:22-23). He spent another 40 years in the desert of relinquishment before he was ready to do things God's way.

EXALTATION AT ONE LEVEL IS ABASEMENT AT A HIGHER.

Moses was "mighty in speech" until he turned 40 and tried to fulfill his destiny on his own. Then he had an intimate encounter with God that apparently left him a stutterer! Sometimes what we consider to be "religious eloquence" is really a "spiritual stutter," an impediment to true communication with and for the Almighty.

Exaltation at one level is abasement at a higher. That is the power of relinquishment. We cannot pray, "Thy kingdom come…" unless first, we are willing to pray, "My kingdom go…."[1] We have a tendency to hold onto "our kingdom" with a death grip, but we need to learn there is a power that comes through relinquishment.

God told His reluctant deliverer, Moses, "When I get through using you, the children of Israel are going to give Me glory. It will not be because of your education, your intelligence, or your ability to speak. *Your leadership ability will not get all the praise for what happens.*" Give man honor, but glory belongs to God alone.

God Never Healed Moses of His Stutter

God performed astounding miracles through Moses, yet as far as we know, God never healed him of his stutter. Sometimes God will leave a mark somewhere on your life as a permanent reminder of the time and place He touched you and changed you forever. It will be a place where He can always get a hold on you.

Moses could tell you about it, if you would be patient with his stuttering delivery. Jacob could tell you about his limp, but you would be able to see that for yourself. So it was with Paul's "thorn in the flesh." Regardless of the strength of his belief in the healing and delivering power of God, we have no record that Paul was healed or delivered of his thorn. It may have been God's means of getting Paul's attention. Paul put it this way:

> *And **lest I should be exalted above measure through the abundance of the revelations**, there was given to me a thorn in the flesh, the messenger of Satan to buffet me, lest I should be exalted above measure. For this thing I besought the Lord thrice, that it might depart from me. And He said unto me, My grace is sufficient for thee: for **My** [God's] **strength is made perfect in weakness**. Most gladly therefore will I rather glory in my infirmities, that the power of Christ may rest upon me (2 Corinthians 12:7-9 KJV, emphasis mine).*

Moses was at the height of his career. He had power, prestige, wealth, and influence with the royal house of Pharaoh. However, he had a prior commitment and a divine commission from the royal house of the Most High God of Israel. He was called of God to deliver the children of Israel from their Egyptian bondage, but first he had to be freed of every shadow of his former house and changed from the heart outward. It took 40 years of shepherding in the wilderness to prepare him for the next 40 years in the place as a deliverer.

Have We Picked Up "Egyptian Shadows"?

Isaiah the prophet spoke of those who "trust in the shadow of Egypt."[2] Some trust in "Egypt" for protection from their enemies, but far more are simply influenced when they get in its shadow. The biblical "shadow of Egypt" shades them from full light. We can pick up "Egyptian shadows" in the biblical sense, though not living as an Egyptian. That was what Moses was doing. This "shadow-proofing" is an unavoidable part of the relinquishment training plan for everyone who is called to exercise leadership at any level in God's Kingdom.

When Moses threw down his favorite old shepherd's rod, it became a serpent and he literally ran from it.[3] Things got worse when God said, "Pick it up by the tail." Nearly everyone knows that is a foolish thing to do because that leaves the "business end" of the snake loose and free for action.

It didn't make much sense to throw down the rod, but it made no sense at all to pick up the snake by the tail! Moses had been in the desert a long time and he knew a poisonous adder when he saw one. But God told him to pick it up by the tail.

Though We Can't "Figure Out" God, We Must Trust Him

During your training trip through the wilderness of relinquishment, you will probably think God is leading you the wrong way, or that He is saying something that doesn't make sense. God's commands aren't always accompanied by explanations. The point is that even when we cannot figure out what God is doing, we must trust Him.

When Moses reluctantly picked up the snake it became a rod again. From this place forward in the narrative, that rod is never again referred to as "the rod of Moses." It is referred to as "the rod of God."[4] Because Moses released it and the snake was taken out of it, it was God's rod. The one thing Moses thought he could trust in the most had to be relinquished to God. God may strip you of everything in order to let you see and understand your total dependence on Him. With that stripping, with that relinquishment, comes power. Sometimes there are things we just want to hold onto that we have to release so God can remove the snake from it.

Our nation is rapidly being conformed to the image of the world, with its many gods and "many paths to salvation." Americans are worshiping demonic power, the occult, pleasure, and even death itself. For more than a decade, many of the top television shows and movies have prominently featured witchcraft, the occult, and the demonic. However, the greatest idol of all on the American scene is the worship of man and of self.

God is looking for something or *someone* to silence these false prophets of the profane. *We need something that will shut the mouths of the gainsayers today*, and it won't happen with better debaters, louder preachers, superior training programs, or larger sound systems. None of these things are bad or evil, but *the only thing that will do it right is the power of God expressed through a selfless life.*

"A Witch Wants to See You..."

Our old friend and prophet of God, T.W. Barnes, received a phone call several years ago from someone who said, "There is a practicing witch in the area who wants to see you. She is the head of a coven of witches." Without hesitation, Pastor Barnes said, "I'll see her!"

As the woman walked into the study where Brother Barnes was waiting for her at the scheduled appointment time, the Lord instantly revealed to him that she had come to leave behind some tormenting spirits. When she sat down, he started talking. The more he talked about the Lord, the more she twisted and squirmed around in her seat. Finally, the lady stood up and started to pace around the room. "I cannot stand it here," she said. "I have to get out." After she left, Pastor Barnes prayed, "Lord, all of those spirits she was bringing to torment me—send them to torment her."

Brother Barnes' phone rang the next morning and it was the same woman he had seen in his study the day before:

"What did you do to me?"

"What do you mean? You weren't even in my office five minutes."

"I was tormented all night long. I couldn't sleep, so I just walked the floor. You did something to me!"

"Yes, I did. I told the Lord to send back the spirits that you brought to torment me. I asked that they would do to you what you wanted them to do to me."

Welcome to Purgatory—Here's Your Bulletin

Do you realize we have authority to torment the devil? Didn't demons speak to Jesus and say, "Have You come here to torment us before the time?" (Mt. 8:29b) *The Church is meant to be the devil's purgatory.* We can torment him while he is still on earth, but first we have to stop looking and living like we belong to him and stop running with his crowd.

Frankly, the wrong group is worried today. The Church shouldn't be worried about the enemy; he should be worried about us! The only reason he isn't very worried is because generally, we are too tame, domesticated, self-centered, and satisfied with mediocrity to be harmful to his health. (God calls it being "lukewarm."[5]).

As long as we keep a tight grip on the way we choose to serve God, we will be about as volatile to the enemy as last week's cold. On the other hand, if we learn the power that comes with relinquishment, we will become a real threat to his kingdom and he will be in real trouble. This is the step beyond salvation and mere church membership. We've signed up in the Lord's army. We've received our notification of acceptance through His blood.

Now it is time for us to board the bus for the ride to boot camp of relinquishment.

The apostle Paul had an encounter with God that completely changed him. When God was finished, that respected Jewish rabbi and scholar let go of his credentials and a bright religious career to follow Christ and declare war on the enemy. One ruler told Paul, "You are beside yourself..." (Acts 26:24b). They were telling him, "You are nuts! You're a fanatic."

Can People Tell You Have Been With Jesus?

Has anyone said that to you lately? (Please understand we are not promoting mere emotionalism.) How long has it been since you were excited about Jesus? Has the glory of God shone through your personal presence recently? Can people feel your presence and marvel that "you've been with Jesus"?[6] We know this happens. By the same token, they can also tell when we have *not* been with Him.

It is too easy for us to bow our knees and not bow our hearts. We cross our fingers behind our backs and pretend that God doesn't see through our performance while we confess total love and loyalty with less-than-total sincerity. The problem is that total relinquishment does not come without a price (and we tend to avoid commitments that require a payment). In God's Kingdom, it is a price worth paying *for there is power with relinquishment.*

You are not a real soldier until you've endured the pain, the discipline, the breaking and remaking that comes in boot camp of relinquishment. The discipline of relinquishment even follows us onto the battlefield at times.

Several years ago a preacher said that the Lord spoke to him during a time of prayer and said:

"I have seen your ministry. Would you like to see Mine?"

The preacher said, "Yes, Lord. What do I have to do?"

God said, *"Give Me back My church."*

The pastor said, "Lord, it *is* Your church."

God replied, *"No. You control everything that is in it. You set the time when the service starts and you dictate when it ends. Worst of all, you control everything in between. I have even heard you call it 'my church.'"*

The pastor repented before the Lord and said, "Lord, it is not my church; it is Your church. I want Your ministry. My ministry at its best is not sufficient at all. I want to see what You can do because what I can do will not get the job done."

The stupidity of independence is as old as Adam and Eve. We must realize that we could not even breathe one breath, think one thought, or earn one dime without His blessing and empowerment. Anything less is presumption and rebellion. *The very taproot of rebellion is in the desire to be "great" on our own terms.* God's treatment and cure for the spirit of independence and rebellion in a believer is the discipline of relinquishment.

Relinquish Man's Stability and Embrace God's Change

Anyone aspiring to leadership in God's Kingdom must learn how to relinquish man's "stability" and embrace God's change, for He is constantly transforming His people in preparation for the great wedding supper of the Lamb. That means change will be our constant companion. Where there is change, there must be relinquishment.

Ask the believers in your church who were born in the 1930s and raised in the 1940s. Change is part of their life story, whether they accepted it or not. They grew up thinking coke was something you drank, not sniffed. It was a time when grass was something cows ate and kids played on. Pot was the kind of pan your Mom cooked with, and hardware was just that. (There was no such thing as "software.") To this day, many of them refuse to give up the original meaning of "gay," which refers to a joyful state of mind, not a sinful sexual preference.

Don't "Miss God" Over a Personal Preference

We are all marked by our musical preferences, and sometimes we live in danger of missing God because of them—especially if He decides to reveal Himself through a music form we have been taught to believe "is of the devil." When people from a "mainline" denomination visit a "Spirit-filled church" for the first time, they are generally shocked to hear everyone pray at one time—and out loud! That is nothing compared to what happens when they hear the people in the congregation sing with great volume and exuberance to "really fast music."

The people from "Spirit-filled churches" face a similar challenge when they visit churches on "the quieter end of God's town." It is hard for them to believe that God could be found in such formal and reserved settings. It is easy to forget that He shows up wherever two or more gather together in His name.

New church settings, methods of worship, and ministry styles tend to invade our "comfort zones," but that doesn't mean these things are "not of God." It is said that our musical preferences are set by the music we enjoy early in our teens. God may want us to relinquish some of our personal tastes and accept the fact that times and people change.

There are new sounds in the Church that are genuine sounds of worship and praise. Don't be surprised if you have to relinquish some of your cherished ideas about what kind of music God likes, or whether or not He likes quiet praise or loud praise. We must be careful to not reject something that is of God simply because it is not reflective of our personal preference.

Release the Form in Favor of the Function

Sometimes we need to relinquish the forms of the past in favor of the present-day function of the Holy Spirit or to accommodate the fresh purposes of God. The Sanhedrin of Jesus' day failed to recognize the very Messiah for whom they had searched all their lives. Why? Because He didn't conform with their self-hallowed forms and presumptions from the past. Those forms began as something good, something godly, and something that was extremely functional for God's purposes. Yet the form was not holy in and of itself. Sometimes we need to lay aside the forms of the past in favor of function.

It all began thousands of years earlier when Moses went into "ministry overload." His time and energy were being depleted by the endless needs of the people. His mental, emotional, physical, and spiritual exhaustion all added up to trouble in the making. Then Jethro, Moses' wise father-in-law, made a little suggestion during a visit. He said, "Moses, it's time to divide the work. Designate it to competent men who fear God and love truth."[7] It was a good form to follow. It actually outlasted Moses and the nation of Israel, but in the process it moved from function to form to Jewish institution.

Many years later in the lifetime of Ezekiel the prophet, this group of delegated judges had become a formal body of 70 judges with great power. Moses and Joshua were gone, and God had sentenced stubborn Israel to judgment. Then God took Ezekiel inside a chamber filled with idols and imagery, with walls that were covered with obscene things.

In the middle of the chamber sat the 70 elders who had evolved from the same system Moses inaugurated five hundred years earlier. They still had the same number, and they were clinging to the same form while practicing abominations instead of truth. God told Ezekiel He was going to judge the nation because of its corrupt judges.[8] Do you see the irony? It gets worse.

The form of the 70 elders survived the Assyrian and Babylonian captivity and reappeared in time. Five hundred years after Ezekiel, when Jesus walked the earth, this group of 70 judges was known as the Sanhedrin. Jesus said the scribes and Pharisees (the two groups dominating the council) "sat in Moses' seat" (Mt. 23:2b). This one council held total power in all Jewish legal, spiritual, and civil matters. They were teachers of the Law and Pharisees. Although they had abandoned the abominations of their predecessors in Ezekiel's day, they had taken on some new abominations of their own.

Slated for a Collision With Christ

In Jesus' day, the form of delegated authority that had served Moses had a life and mission of its own. It primarily existed to give 70 men a prestigious position and career in the Jewish community. The form had gone far astray of its original function and was slated for a head-on collision with the Messiah, Jesus Christ.

These men didn't realize that Jesus didn't come to die just so someone could have a "position and career." They had forgotten that ministry is a compassion and a divine calling, not a career. The members of the Sanhedrin viewed Jesus as an embarrassing thorn and problem *until Lazarus was raised from the dead.* This miracle was too great and too widely known to talk away, and the Sanhedrin was called together to deal with the problem:

> *Then the chief priests and the Pharisees gathered a council and said, "What shall we do? For this Man works many signs. If we let Him alone like this, everyone will believe in Him, and the Romans will come and* **take away both our place** *and nation."...Then, from that day on, they plotted to put Him to death....[They] plotted to put Lazarus to death also, because on account of him many of the Jews went away and believed in Jesus* (John 11:47-48,53; 12:10-11).

When the *religious form* decided that Jesus was a threat to their *status-quo*, the form decided to kill the Way, the Truth, and the Life of God. Something that had started out as a good function with Moses had become so self-serving that it became a weight and encumbrance to God Himself.

Form Without Mission Is Lifeless Tradition

What was once a blessing had become a burden. Function calls for form, but so often, once forms are put in place they tend to become virtually indestructible. They live on and on and on long after their original function and purpose has been lost. Once mission is lost in form, all you have left is a lifeless tradition of man or a cultural custom. If the pattern holds true, it soon becomes "heretical" to even question the form. That is what happened with the 70. The form outlived its day of usefulness and instead became a trapping of tradition.

Consider the progression: When Moses established the 70 judges, they were a strength and blessing of God to him and the people. By Ezekiel's time they had become evil-thinkers and evil-doers. In Jesus' day, the Sanhedrin was so spiritually out of touch that they did not recognize the Messiah they studied in the Scriptures, and they condemned the Son of God to death.

COULD IT BE THAT WEIGHTS AND FORMS WE REFUSE TO LAY ASIDE BECOME THE SINS THAT SO EASILY BESET US?

Moses had to learn two things about the rod: You *relinquish* it when God says let go, and you *pick it up* when He says pick it up. If he failed to obey either one of these simple commands, he could lose everything. In fact, he failed the test once in the wilderness.

God told Moses to *speak to the rock* and it would yield its water to the thirsty.[9] This prefigured the day Christ the Rock would cry out in Jerusalem:

On the last day, that great day of the feast, Jesus stood and cried out, saying, "If anyone thirsts, let him come to Me and drink. He who believes in Me, as the Scripture has said, out of his heart will flow rivers of living water" (John 7:37-38).

IS THERE A REVERSE POWER OR NEGATIVE ENERGY THAT COMES FROM NOT LEARNING THE POWER OF RELINQUISHMENT?

Moses instead took up God's rod of life and used it as a rod of anger and struck the Rock of Salvation, which symbolized the Christ of the future. That simple but serious mistake cost Moses his right to enter the promised land.

One of the most important roles of the Sanhedrin was to explain and interpret the laws of Moses. By that time, the religious leaders had *added* 1,500 regulations to the basic Law of Moses just to "protect the sanctity" or religiosity of the Sabbath. It was something that needed to be relinquished and unloaded. It was form that had lost its true function.

The solution is to plug into the things of the Spirit. We must be willing to relinquish any "form" that does not *conform* to the present purposes of God and eternal truths of His revealed Word. This is especially important in those times when it is clear that God is doing a new thing in and among His people.

God Is Committed to Character, Not Talent

What is in your hand? Ability? A fine mind? Power to influence people? Eloquence? Personality? Talent? Throw it down—there might be a snake in it! Regardless of our personal talents and abilities, God is committed to character, not talent. He wants us to be totally dependent on Him. What is in your hand? Let God have it. There could be a little sin left in it. A little serpent life might be there that you don't even know about.

We must take our gifts—whatever they may be—and cast them at the feet of Jesus. Let Him take the serpent—the flesh—out of them and give them back to us. Then they become the power of God in our lives. Where leadership is concerned, that even includes the "approval" of the people you lead. Leadership can be lonely at times, and misunderstanding seems to be part of the leadership package. Even Jesus had to live with misunderstanding throughout His earthly ministry, and after all, He was *perfect*. The rest of us should expect to run into some problems that call for even more relinquishment along the way.

Moses didn't fit the stereotype of a great leader. His first attempt to help his people led to murder, rejection by the Hebrews, and a frantic flight into the wilderness. To say he was totally misunderstood might be an understatement. The misunderstanding became stronger the longer the Israelites marched through the wilderness.

Finally, a Levite leader named Korah rose up with 250 top Israelite leaders and publicly challenged Moses' leadership. Moses fell to the ground and humbly buried his face in the sand, and God showed up in righteous anger and instantly buried Korah and his cohorts in the sand. Those men didn't understand that Moses' power came from his humble relinquishment of *everything* to the Lord.[10] Moses also knew what it was like to have his own family misunderstand him. Miriam and Aaron, his older sister and brother, even tried to usurp his authority one time, but once again God stepped in and settled the matter.[11] Sometimes those closest to you—your own family—will be the ones who misunderstand.

Why did Jesse bring all his sons *except David* when the prophet invited him to a sacrifice *with his sons?*[12] David wrote,

"Behold, I was brought forth in iniquity, and in sin my mother conceived me" (Ps. 51:5). It is interesting that this is the only mention of David's mother in the Bible, other than when he asked the King of Moab for asylum for his "father and mother" (I Sam. 22:3).

Relinquish Your History to the Past

Have you ever wondered if David was an illegitimate child? Perhaps his father did not consider him to be one of his true sons. It is just a thought, but if it is true, then it only reinforces the power of relinquishment. This is the power that helped David leave his history in his past! God has been known to take the downcast and illegitimate and make them legitimate!

God saw past the surface and peered into David's heart. When young David told King Saul he would go out to meet Goliath in battle, he didn't brag, "Watch how good my aim is!" He didn't even mention the slingshot and the five smooth stones or the fact that he had just enough "ammunition" for Goliath. He just said, "The Lord, who delivered me from the paw of the lion and from the paw of the bear, He will deliver me from the hand of this Philistine" (1 Sam. 17:37a).

Oddly enough, The Amplified Version says David put the stones in his lunch bag![13] He wasn't going to a fight; he was en route to a picnic. Goliath bragged, "I'm going to eat your lunch," but little did he know what was in David's lunch bag. David was willing to let go—to relinquish himself—to the glory of God, and miracles happened. (In a sense, David was the first "rock and roller"—He rocked Goliath and the giant rolled!)

The Divine Delay Between Anointing and Appointing

David also knew what it was to be misunderstood because of the anointing on his life, and because of the *divine delay* between the revelation of anointing and the appointment to that anointing. When the prophet of God came looking for God's replacement for King Saul, Samuel passed over all his older brothers and then, *right in front of them all*, he anointed David to be king over Israel. What happened next was exactly nothing.

The prophet left town and the youngest boy in the family returned to the back pasture. As for his brothers, we can safely presume that once the prophet left, they didn't bow down to David; they laughed and mocked him mercilessly. God had anointed David to be king in Saul's place, but he had to return to the sheep and "hurry up and wait." He didn't run through the land proclaiming, "I'm going to be king!" He went back to the sheepfold and took care of his father's sheep as if they would be his responsibility for a lifetime. This is the proper way to relinquish to the Lord the times and seasons of your life.

David knew he was anointed, and so did God and His prophet. This young shepherd-warrior just kept praying and singing to God, waiting and watching the sheep (while killing a few large predators along the way). Then someone in King Saul's court recognized David's gifts in worship and warfare.[14] Finally, David's anointing hit Goliath right between the eyes, and all of Israel, Judah, and Philistia knew it.[15]

Relinquish Your Right to Hurry God

Sometimes God shows you something that will come to pass in the future. If it's not time for it, don't run through the camp shouting, "I'm anointed!" Make sure you relinquish your "right" to hurry God along or to help Him plan out your destiny. He doesn't need our help. God's promises are not tied to time. They are tied to God alone, and He is timeless. He can do a quick work.

If you feel discouraged in this area, remember Moses. When he obeyed God and extended the rod over the Red Sea, the waves split open and the children of Israel walked across to victory.

That sounds nice, doesn't it? Now do the math and take courage in God's ability to "hurry things along" when He is ready to do so.

There were between three and five million Israelites, so God didn't struggle to provide a few muddy single-file footpaths for those people. If the Israelites crossed that distance in one night, then they marched five thousand abreast (side by side) along a dry, smooth roadway the width of a 48-lane highway! God opened up the largest freeway in history to get millions of Israelites across the Red Sea, and He did it in a brief period of time. When God gets ready, He can do a quick work. *God delivered the Israelites from four hundred years of bondage in one night!* The Bible says they were "baptized into Moses."[16] What a revival! How would you like to see three-to-five million baptized in one night?

God always seems to be interested in what is in our hands. "Mary, what is in your hand?" "An alabaster box of ointment." She broke it open and cast the pieces at the feet of Jesus and now for two thousand years we've been smelling it in the air. That is what release and relinquishment did for her. It was a lasting memorial to Jesus' death on the cross.

No one else noticed, but Jesus saw what was in the widow's hand when she dropped her last two mites into the offering plate. He honored her as an example of the kind of sacrificial giving God loves to bless, and her example has been utilized to build the faith of believers and raise millions of dollars for the Kingdom of God over the centuries. It was all because this widow took what was in her hand and relinquished it to the Lord by faith. Like the song says, "Little is much when God is in it."

We must have the spirit of selflessness manifested in the prayers Jesus taught us to pray and modeled before us: "Nevertheless not My will, but Yours, be done" (Lk.22:42b). "Your kingdom come. Your will be done on earth as it is in Heaven" (Mt. 6:10).

Relinquish What You Have to Him

God is not looking for exceptionally talented, educated, or gifted people. These qualities are certainly admirable and beneficial, but they are not required. What he is looking for is men and women who are willing to relinquish whatever they have to Him. Release your "staff" to Him. He will take the serpent out of it and give it back to you. It then becomes the rod of God. We will never comprehend this until we humble ourselves and let God make out of us what He wants us to be.

Moses never pictured himself spending 40 years in a desert. When God revealed that he was to be a deliverer, he was ready to "get the show on the road." But God said, "Wait. I've got something for you to learn first." There are seasons of life. God sometimes puts things in our hearts prior to the time for their fulfillment. We cannot rush the seasons. We must relinquish the times of our life to Him who holds them in His hand.

Moses did several things with his rod. He led the Israelites out of bondage. He led them out of barrenness. He led them out as he parted the Red Sea. It was the same rod. But he had to take his own hand off of it first. It had to become the rod of God.

Too often we think there is power in holding on. The laws of the Kingdom are in reverse. We must turn loose. Jesus wants us to tell Him, "Lord, take me and use me. Wherever You want me to go, whoever You want me to speak to, whatever You want me to do—I am Yours." Total relinquishment of self will bring God's power into your life. This is the power of relinquishment.

Relinquish What You Don't Understand to Him

It was this power that enabled the men of the New Testament to walk into hostile cities virtually alone. On one such occasion, the Lord told the apostle Paul, "I have many people in this city" (Acts 18:10b). There wasn't one convert at the time, but God saw something Paul could not see and he had to trust God all the way. The power of relinquishment is the ability to relinquish what we don't understand to a divine mandate. We do not want to walk away from a place in which God sees potential. Where He leads, we must follow, and He will receive all the glory.

Arturo Tuscani was a famous Italian symphony conductor. His specialty was the works of Beethoven. One night in Philadelphia, Pennsylvania, Tuscani conducted the Philadelphia Symphony Orchestra in a program that included the Ninth Symphony, one of the most difficult pieces to direct. It was so majestic and so moving that when the piece was completed, the audience stood for round after round of applause. Tuscani took his bows again and again. He turned to the orchestra; they bowed. The audience continued to clap and cheer. The orchestra members themselves were smiling and clapping. Finally, Tuscani turned his back to the audience, and spoke only to the orchestra. He said, "Ladies, gentlemen—I am nothing. You are nothing. Beethoven is everything."

When you think of this story, remember the divine power of relinquishment. Regardless of how eloquent you are, or how gifted you are with a voice to sing like an angel, *throw yourself at the feet of Jesus and let Him take the serpent out of your gift.*

When men first learned to navigate the open seas using the stars as their "road map," a whole new world opened up to them. Until the development of state-of-the-art satellite positioning technology, the compass was the primary instrument of navigation at sea. It was said, *"He who is a slave to the compass enjoys the freedom of the open sea."*

Commitment to the compass of God opens the door of the universe to us. When you commit your future to God and let Him set your course, He will direct you to places of unprecedented freedom and usefulness in the Kingdom. First, you must be willing to say with the apostle Paul, "…it is no longer I who live, but

Christ lives in me" (Gal. 2:20a). Declare to Him, "I am nothing. You are everything. Here I am, and here are my gifts, abilities, and dreams, Lord. I throw it all down at Your feet. I give You all, and I hold nothing back."

Endnotes

1. See Mt. 6:10.
2. See Is. 30:2-3.
3. See Ex. 4:3-4.
4. See Ex. 4:1-20 and Ex. 17:9.
5. See Rev. 3:15-18.
6. See Acts 4:13.
7. An abbreviated paraphrase of Ex. 18:21.
8. See Ezek. 8:11-12,18.
9. See Num. 20:8.
10. See Num. 16.
11. See Num. 12.
12. See 1 Sam. 16:11.
13. See 1 Sam. 17:40, key words cited from *The Amplified Bible* (Grand Rapids, Michigan: Zondervan Publishing House and the Lockman Foundation, 1987).
14. See 1 Sam. 16:18.
15. See 1 Sam. 17:45-52.
16. See 1 Cor. 10:2.

Devil Shrinking 101

The Classroom of the Spirit

Come with me now into the classroom of the Holy Spirit. The course of study includes a "workbook," a "laboratory" for experiments and yes, there will be a test! But do not make this a "crash course." Rather, take your time and learn how to rise above any and every opposing circumstance in your life. There will be difficult times of testing. You will be tried and proven, but there is genuine hope for success. Many students before you have graduated from this course with flying colors. One of the early graduates wrote:

> *For I am now ready to be offered, and the time of my departure is at hand. I have fought a good fight, I have finished my course, I have kept the faith: Henceforth there is laid up for me a crown of righteousness, which the Lord, the righteous judge, shall give me at that day: and not to me only, but unto all them also that love His appearing* (2 Timothy 4:6-8).

There will also be a diploma given upon the successful completion of your course of study. Each student will receive a plaque of recognition with the engraved words, "Well done, good and faithful servant" (Mt. 25:23). And the person handing out the diplomas and recognition will be the Creator of the universe, the King of kings and the Victor over death, hell, and the grave. He has been given all power in Heaven and earth. He is the man who carries the keys to hell. That's right, contrary to what some people believe, the devil does not even have the keys to his own house!

This little study guide, *Honey, I Shrunk the devil*, and the official textbook, the Holy Bible, can assist and equip you in completing your course of study. Other students in the class may discuss ideas and encourage you, but you will have to do your own work. To complete this class successfully you will need to work out your own deliverance. As a teacher's assistant, my goal for each student is simply "…that they may recover themselves out of the snare of the devil, who are taken captive by him at his will" (2 Tim. 2:26).

Before we begin our coursework, let's note that there are two primary facts about the world in which we live—there is a God and there is a devil. There is also one primary question each person will at some point answer: Who is bigger?

While there is no question who is actually greater in the universe and who will ultimately reign supreme, human perception varies from person to person. This perception determines to what degree a person will conquer and overcome his or her enemies. Some people see the devil as being too big for God to handle, let alone someone they themselves can conquer. For those who see or fear the "big monster," I offer a practical plan to shrink the devil. Together we can make him small enough to stomp! For those who have already discovered how to minimize the enemy, these pages will help to keep him small and not allow him to grow in their lives! Now, let's get down to business with some basic principles.

HONEY I SHRUNK THE DEVIL!
by Dianne Sloan
ISBN 0-7684-3026-7

Available at your local Christian bookstore.

GodChasers.network

GodChasers.network is the ministry of Tommy and Jeannie Tenney. Their heart's desire is to see the presence and power of God fall—not just in churches, but on cities and communities all over the world.

How to contact us:

By Mail:

> GodChasers.network
> **P.O. Box 3355**
> **Pineville, Louisiana 71361**
> **USA**

By Phone:

Voice:	318.44CHASE (318.442.4273)
Fax:	318.442.6884
Orders:	888.133.3355

By Internet:

E-mail:	Contact@GodChasers.net
Website:	www.GodChasers.net

Join Today

When you join the **GodChasers.network** we'll send you a free teaching tape!

If you share in our vision and want to stay current on how the Lord is using GodChasers.network, please add your name to our mailing list. We'd like to keep you updated on what the Spirit is saying through Tommy. We'll also send schedule updates and make you aware of new resources as they become available.

Sign up by calling or writing to (U.S. residents only):

> **Tommy Tenney**
> **GodChasers.network**
> **P.O. Box 3355**
> **Pineville, Louisiana 71361-3355**
> **USA**
>
> **318-44CHASE (318.442.4273)**
> **or sign up online at**
> **http://www.GodChasers.net/lists/**

We regret that we are only able to send regular postal mailings to US residents at this time. If you live outside the US you can still add your postal address to our mailing list—you will automatically begin to receive our mailings as soon as they are available in your area.

E-mail Announcement List

If you'd like to receive information from us via e-mail, join our E-mail Announcement List by visiting our website at www.GodChasers.net/lists/.

"Chase God" with us Online!

The **GodChasers.network** is proud to bring you some of the most family-friendly Internet access available today! We've partnered with some Internet leaders to provide state-of-the art facilities, national and international dialup coverage, and 24-hour technical support. This is truly the best that the Internet has to offer: a service that is both reliable and safe! We use the industry's ONLY true artificial intelligence filter, the BAIR™ filtering System, so you can surf the net in a wholesome environment!

Features:

- Exclusive GodChasers.network Content
- Email address: Yourname@GodChasers.net
- Chat channels with opportunities to talk with Tommy and Jeannie Tenney, GodChasers staff, and guests
- Artificial Intelligence text and picture filtering
- Full Internet Capabilities
- Instant messaging
- Streaming audio/video
- Download MP3 Music files
- Much Much More!

For more information or to sign up today, you can visit our web site at **http://www.GodChasers.com/**. You can also call or write to us to receive software by mail!

Run With Us!

Become a GodChasers.network Monthly Seed Partner

"Have you caught Him yet?"

We're asked a lot of questions like that— and with a name like "God-Chasers.network," we've come to expect it! Do we really think that we can "catch" God? Is God running away from us? What are we talking about?

"God chasers" are people whose hunger for Him compels them to run—not walk—towards a deeper and more meaningful relationship with the Almighty. For them, it isn't just a casual pursuit. Sundays and Wednesday nights aren't enough: they need Him every day, in every situation and circumstance, the good times and the bad.

Chasing God in our troubled times isn't always easy, but if we're really seeking God, and not just His blessings, then our cicumstances shouldn't hinder our pursuit. We will find God in trying times and learn that He is in control even when everything around us seems to be spinning out of control. He may *seem* distant from us...but when we pursue Him, we'll find that He *wants* us to "catch" Him, and He will draw near. That's what "chasing God" is all about!

Are you a "God chaser"? If the cries of your heart are echoed in the words of this message, would you prayerfully consider "running with us" as a GodChasers.network partner? Each month, our Seed Partners who sow into this ministry with a monthly gift of $20 or more receive a teaching tape. It's a small token of our gratitude, and helps our partners stay current with the direction and flow of the ministry.

Thank you for your interest in **GodChasers.network**. We look forward to chasing Him with you!

In Pursuit,

Tommy Tenney

Tommy Tenney
& The GodChasers.network Staff

Become a Monthly Seed Partner
by calling or writing to:

Tommy Tenney
GodChasers.network
P.O. Box 3355
Pineville, Louisiana 71361-3355
318.44CHASE (318.442.4273)

4 TT

AUDIOTAPE ALBUMS BY TOMMY TENNEY

FANNING THE FLAMES

(audiotape album) $20 plus $4.50 S&H

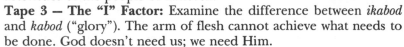

Tape 1 — The Application of the Blood and the Ark of the Covenant: Most of the churches in America today dwell in an outer-court experience. Jesus made atonement with His own blood, once for all, and the veil in the temple was rent from top to bottom.

Tape 2 — A Tale of Two Cities—Nazareth & Nineveh: Jesus spent more time in Nazareth than any other city, yet there was great resistance to the works of God there. In contrast, consider the characteristics of the people of Nineveh.

Tape 3 — The "I" Factor: Examine the difference between *ikabod* and *kabod* ("glory"). The arm of flesh cannot achieve what needs to be done. God doesn't need us; we need Him.

KEYS TO LIVING THE REVIVED LIFE

(audiotape album) $20 plus $4.50 S&H

Tape 1 - Fear Not: The principles that Tommy reveals teach us that to have no fear is to have faith, and that perfect love casts out fear, so we establish the trust of a child in our loving Father.

Tape 2 - Hanging in There: Have you ever been tempted to give up, quit, and throw in the towel? This message is a word of encouragement for you. Everybody has a place and a position in the Kingdom of God. Jeannie Tenney joins her husband and sings an inspiring chorus, "I'm Going Through."

Tape 3 - Fire of God: Fire purges the sewer of our souls and destroys the hidden things that would cause disease. Learn the way out of a repetitive cycle of seasonal times of failure.

NEW!
GOD'S DREAM TEAM AUDIO SERIES

(audiotape album) $20 plus $4.50 S&H

Only we can answer the only unanswered prayer of Jesus. "That they may be one!" This collection contains three of Tommy's messages on unity.

TURNING ON THE LIGHT
OF THE GLORY

(video) $20 plus $4.50 S&H

Tommy deals with turning on the light of the glory and presence of God, and he walks us through the necessary process and ingredients to potentially unleash what His Body has always dreamed of.

To order any of the products listed on these pages, receive information concerning the ministry of Tommy Tenney, or to join the GodChasers.network, please contact:

GodChasers.network
P.O. Box 3355
Pineville, LA 71361
318-44CHASE (318.442.4273)
888.433.3355
Fax: 318.442.6884
www.GodChasers.net
GodChaser@GodChasers.net

More titles
by Tommy Tenney

THE GOD CHASERS (National Best-Seller)
There are those so hungry, so desperate for His presence, that they become consumed with finding Him. Their longing for Him moves them to do what they would otherwise never do: Chase God. But what does it really mean to chase God? Can He be "caught"? Is there an end to the thirsting of man's soul for Him? Meet Tommy Tenney—God chaser. Join him in his search for God. Follow him as he ignores the maze of religious tradition and finds himself, not chasing God, but to his utter amazement, caught by the One he had chased.
ISBN 0-7684-2016-4
Also available in Spanish
ISBN 0-7899-0642-2

**GOD CHASERS DAILY MEDITATION
& PERSONAL JOURNAL**
Does your heart yearn to have an intimate relationship with your Lord? Perhaps you long to draw closer to your heavenly Father, but you don't know how or where to start. This *Daily Meditation & Personal Journal* will help you begin a journey that will change your life. As you read and journal, you'll find your spirit running to meet Him with a desire and fervor you've never before experienced. Let your heart hunger propel you into the chase of your life...after God!
ISBN 0-7684-2040-7

GOD'S FAVORITE HOUSE
The burning desire of your heart can be fulfilled. God is looking for people just like you. He is a Lover in search of a people who will love Him in return. He is far more interested in you than He is interested in a building. He would hush all of Heaven's hosts to listen to your voice raised in heartfelt love songs to Him. This book will show you how to build a house of worship within, fulfilling your heart's desire and His!
ISBN 0-7684-2043-1

Available at your local Christian bookstore.

For more information and sample chapters,
visit www.reapernet.com

6B-1:32

Other books endorsed
by Tommy Tenney

▬ **DIGGING THE WELLS OF REVIVAL by Lou Engle**

Foreword—Within our history lies our hope. *Digging the Wells of Revival* draws our attention to the spiritual inheritance of our country. From Azusa Street in Los Angeles at the turn of the century, to Toronto, Baltimore, and Brownsville as we face the next century, Lou Engle reminds us that what was, can be what is—where waters once flowed freely, they can again spring forth in this generation.
ISBN 0-7684-2015-6

▬ **A DIVINE CONFRONTATION by Graham Cooke**

Foreword—If you choose to read this book, you should probably throw out your old ecclesiastical dictionary. Nothing is as it seems…it's bigger and better. Only we didn't know it! And Graham Cooke told us. Change is coming! The spiritual climate is about to be radically altered. Thank you, Graham, for "forthtelling" the spiritual weather patterns.
ISBN 0-7684-2039-3

▬ **THEY DRANK FROM THE RIVER AND DIED IN THE WILDERNESS by David Ravenhill**

Foreword—Move from the place of *privilege* to the place of *purpose*, from the people of God *among* the nations, to the priests of God *to* the nations. The river is not the goal! It's a "gate"! Cross and enter—God's promises are in the promised land! Wildness is in the wilderness! The wilderness is only the *bridge* between slavery and sonship—Egypt and Canaan. Don't die en route!
ISBN 0-7684-2038-5

▬ **NO MORE SOUR GRAPES by Don Nori**

Don Nori has masterfully passed on to us the lessons of true fatherhood. He states powerfully: "The children's deliverance is locked up in the parents' repentance." Amen, Father Don! I agree! I repent! *No more sour grapes!*
ISBN 0-7684-2037-7

▬ **THE LOST PASSIONS OF JESUS by Donald L. Milam, Jr.**

This book is on fire! To be left unchanged you'd havc to read it with asbestos gloves and an iceberg heart.
ISBN 0-9677402-0-7

Available at your local Christian bookstore.

For more information and sample chapters, visit www.reapernet.com

6B-1:8

Other books endorsed
by Tommy Tenney

━━━ FATHER, FORGIVE US! by Jim W. Goll
This book is a road map to restoring the power and passion of forgiveness. How could we have neglected it so long? *Father, forgive us!*
ISBN 0-7684-2025-3

━━━ THE RELEASE OF THE HUMAN SPIRIT by Frank Houston
The bindings on this book cover must be extra strong! That's the only thing I know that keeps this book from 'exploding'! Are you ready to release your spirit? To go to the next level?
ISBN 0-7684-2019-9

━━━ THE MARTYRS' TORCH by Bruce Porter
The Body of Christ will be eternally grateful for what the pastor and parents of Rachel Scott share in this book. "There shall be light at evening time" (see Zech. 14:7b). We can see the future by the bright light of *The Martyrs' Torch*.
ISBN 0-7684-2046-6

━━━ THE RADICAL CHURCH by Bryn Jones
He calls for a heavenly harmony where earth begins to sing on pitch with heaven's tune...where man prays the Lord's prayers instead of man's prayers. In Bryn's words, "Is it not time for passionate prophetic confrontation again?"
ISBN 0-7684-2022-9

━━━ POWER, HOLINESS, AND EVANGELISM by Randy Clark
The future of the Church is at stake and this book has some answers. These authors speak eloquently, confirming what you have felt, affirming what you intuitively knew.
ISBN 1-56043-345-0

Available at your local Christian bookstore.

For more information and sample chapters, visit www.reapernet.com

6B-1:9

More
GOD CHASER
Products!

GOD CHASER HAT
GCH $17.99

GOD CHASER SHIRT

(M)	GCT-M	$16.99
(L)	GCT-L	$16.99
(XL)	GCT-XL	$16.99
(2X)	GCT-2XL	$18.99

GOD CHASER
LICENSE PLATE
GCLP $6.99

Available at your local Christian bookstore.

**For more information
visit www.reapernet.com**

Books to help you grow strong in Jesus

⬤ TODAY GOD IS FIRST
by Os Hillman.
Sometimes it is hard to keep Him first in my day. It is a struggle to see Him in the circumstances of my job. I need help to bring the reality of my Lord into my place of work. Os Hillman has the uncanny ability to write just to my circumstance, exactly to my need. He helps me see God's view. He strengthens my faith and courage to both see God and invite Him into the everyday trials and struggles of work. Take this book to work, put it on your desk or table. Every day just before you tackle the mountains before you, pause long enough to remind yourself—Today, God is First.
ISBN 0-7684-2049-0

⬤ THE ASCENDED LIFE
by Bernita J. Conway.
A believer does not need to wait until Heaven to experience an intimate relationship with the Lord. When you are born again, your life becomes His, and He pours His life into yours. Here Bernita Conway explains from personal study and experience the truth of "abiding in the Vine," the Lord Jesus Christ. When you grasp this understanding and begin to walk in it, it will change your whole life and relationship with your heavenly Father!
ISBN 1-56043-337-X

⬤ EXTRAORDINARY POWER FOR ORDINARY CHRISTIANS
by Erik Tammaru.
Ordinary people don't think too much about extraordinary power. We think that this kind of power is for extraordinary people. We forget that it is this supernatural power that makes us all extraordinary! We are all special in His sight and we all have the hope of extraordinary living. His power can change ordinary lives into lives empowered by the Holy Spirit and directed by His personal love for us.
ISBN 1-56043-309-1

⬤ THE THRESHOLD OF GLORY
compiled by Dotty Schmitt.
What does it mean to experience the "glory of God"? How does it come? These women of God have crossed that threshold, and it changed not only their ministries but also their very lives! Here Dotty Schmitt and Sue Ahn, Bonnie Chavda, Pat Chen, Dr. Flo Ellers, Brenda Kilpatrick, and Varle Rollins teach about God's glorious presence and share how it transformed their lives.
ISBN 0-7684-2044-X

Available at your local Christian bookstore.

For more information and sample chapters, visit www.reapernet.com

6B-1:11

Books to help you grow strong in Jesus

▬▬ THE HIDDEN POWER OF PRAYER AND FASTING
by Mahesh Chavda.
The praying believer is the confident believer. But the fasting believer is the overcoming believer. This is the believer who changes the circumstances and the world around him. He is the one who experiences the supernatural power of the risen Lord in his everyday life. An international evangelist and the senior pastor of All Nations Church in Charlotte, North Carolina, Mahesh Chavda has seen firsthand the power of God released through a lifestyle of prayer and fasting. Here he shares from decades of personal experience and scriptural study principles and practical tips about fasting and praying. This book will inspire you to tap into God's power and change your life, your city, and your nation!
ISBN 0-7684-2017-2

▬▬ THE LOST ART OF INTERCESSION
by Jim W. Goll.
Finally there is something that really explains what is happening to so many folk in the Body of Christ. What does it mean to carry the burden of the Lord? Where is it in Scripture and in history? Why do I feel as though God is groaning within me? No, you are not crazy; God is restoring genuine intercessory prayer in the hearts of those who are open to respond to His burden and His passion.
ISBN 1-56043-697-2

▬▬ ENCOUNTERING THE PRESENCE
by Colin Urquhart.
What is it about Jesus that, when we encounter Him, we are changed? When we encounter the Presence, we encounter the Truth, because Jesus is the Truth. Here Colin Urquhart, best-selling author and pastor in Sussex, England, explains how the Truth changes facts. Do you desire to become more like Jesus? The Truth will set you free!
ISBN 0-7684-2018-0

▬▬ WORSHIP: THE PATTERN OF THINGS IN HEAVEN
by Joseph L. Garlington.
Worship and praise play a crucial role in the local church. Whether you are a pastor, worship leader, musician, or lay person, you'll find rich and anointed teaching from the Scriptures about worship! Joseph L. Garlington, Sr., a pastor, worship leader, and recording artist in his own right, shows how *worship is the pattern of things in Heaven*!
ISBN 1-56043-195-4

▬▬ RELEASERS OF LIFE
by Mary Audrey Raycroft.
Inside you is a river that is waiting to be tapped—the river of the Holy Spirit and power! Let Mary Audrey Raycroft, a gifted exhorter and teacher and the Pastor of Equipping Ministries and Women in Ministry at the Toronto Airport Christian Fellowship, teach you how you can release the unique gifts and anointings that the Lord has placed within you. Discover how you can move and minister in God's freeing power and be a releaser of life!
ISBN 1-56043-198-9

Available at your local Christian bookstore.

6B-1:12

Books to help you grow strong in Jesus

LADY IN WAITING

by Debby Jones and Jackie Kendall.

This is not just another book for single women! The authors, both well-known conference speakers, present an in-depth study on the biblical Ruth that reveals the characteristics every woman of God should develop. Learn how you can become a lady of faith, purity, contentment, patience—and much more—as you pursue a personal and intimate relationship with your Lord Jesus!

ISBN 1-56043-848-7

Devotional Journal and Study Guide

ISBN 1-56043-298-5

FROM THE FATHER'S HEART

by Charles Slagle.

This is a beautiful look at the true heart of your heavenly Father. Through these sensitive selections that include short love notes, letters, and prophetic words from God to His children, you will develop the kind of closeness and intimacy with the loving Father that you have always longed for. From words of encouragement and inspiration to words of gentle correction, each letter addresses times that we all experience. For those who diligently seek God, you will recognize Him in these pages.

ISBN 0-914903-82-9

AN INVITATION TO FRIENDSHIP: From the Father's Heart, Volume 2

by Charles Slagle.

Our God is a Father whose heart longs for His children to sit and talk with Him in fellowship and oneness. This second volume of intimate letters from the Father to you, His child, reveals His passion, dreams, and love for you. As you read them, you will find yourself drawn ever closer within the circle of His embrace. The touch of His presence will change your life forever!

ISBN 0-7684-2013-X

DON'T DIE IN THE WINTER...

by Dr. Millicent Thompson.

Why do we go through hard times? Why must we suffer pain? In *Don't Die in the Winter...* Dr. Thompson, a pastor, teacher, and conference speaker, explains the spiritual seasons and cycles that people experience. A spiritual winter is simply a season that tests our growth. We need to endure our winters, for in the plan of God, spring always follows winter!

ISBN 1-56043-558-5

UNDERSTANDING THE DREAMS YOU DREAM

by Ira Milligan.

Have you ever had a dream in which you think God was speaking to you? Here is a practical guide, from the Christian perspective, for understanding the symbolic language of dreams. Deliberately written without technical jargon, this book can be easily understood and used by everyone. Includes a complete dictionary of symbols.

ISBN 1-56043-284-5

Available at your local Christian bookstore.

For more information and sample chapters, visit www.reapernet.com

6B-1:13

Exciting titles
by Bill Hamon

━━ APOSTLES, PROPHETS AND THE COMING MOVES OF GOD

Author of the "Prophets" series, Dr. Bill Hamon brings the same anointed instruction in this new series on apostles! Learn about the apostolic age and how apostles and prophets work together. Find out God's end-time plans for the Church!
ISBN 0-939868-09-1

━━ PROPHETS AND PERSONAL PROPHECY

This book defines the role of a prophet or prophetess and gives the reader strategic guidelines for judging prophecy. Many of the stories included are taken from Dr. Bill's ministry and add that "hands on" practicality that is quickly making this book a best-seller.
ISBN 0-939868-03-2

━━ PROPHETS AND THE PROPHETIC MOVEMENT

This sequel to *Prophets and Personal Prophecy* is packed with the same kind of cutting instruction that made the first volume a best-seller. Prophetic insights, how-to's, and warnings make this book essential for the Spirit-filled church.
ISBN 0-939868-04-0

━━ PROPHETS, PITFALLS, AND PRINCIPLES

This book shows you how to recognize your hidden "root" problems, and detect and correct character flaws and "weed seed" attitudes. It also can teach you how to discern true prophets using Dr. Hamon's ten M's.
ISBN 0-939868-05-9

Available at your local Christian bookstore.

Books to help you grow strong in Jesus

━ ONLY BELIEVE
by Don Stewart.
Who was A.A. Allen, John Dowie, Maria Woodworth-Etter, and William Branham? Who were these and the many other people who picked up the mantle of the healing evangelist in the twentieth century? What was their legacy? Don Stewart, who was mentored by A.A. Allen and had contact with most of his contemporaries in this widespread movement, gives an inside look into their lives and ministries. This incredible, firsthand witness account of the events and people who have shaped our current Christian heritage will astound you with how God takes frail, human vessels, pours out His anointing, and enables them to do mighty exploits for Him!
ISBN 1-56043-340-X

━ THE HOUSE OF HIS CHOOSING...
by Jim Wies.
What is your understanding of the foundation of today's Church? The insights in this book will help you view the Church and how it works in a whole new way!
ISBN 0-7684-2041-5

━ MIRACLE OF THE SCARLET THREAD
by Richard Booker.
From Genesis to Revelation, the scarlet thread is woven through every book of the Bible. This worldwide, best-selling classic unravels the complexities of explaining God's blood covenant with man. It sheds light on the Old Testament and demonstrates how the Old and New Testaments fit perfectly together to tell one complete story. This book is considered standard reading for churches, study groups, and Bible schools around the world!
ISBN 0-914903-26-8

━ WHEN THE HEAVENS ARE BRASS
by John Kilpatrick.
Pastor John Kilpatrick wanted something more. He began to pray, but it seemed like the heavens were brass. The lessons he learned over the years helped birth a mighty revival in Brownsville Assembly of God that is sweeping through this nation and the world. The dynamic truths in this book could birth life-changing revival in your own life and ministry!
ISBN 1-56043-190-3

Available at your local Christian bookstore.

6B-1:20

Books to help you grow strong in Jesus